the MOCKINGBIRD
PARABLES

the MOCKINGBIRD
PARABLES

Matt Litton

THOMAS NELSON
Since 1798

NASHVILLE   DALLAS   MEXICO CITY   RIO DE JANEIRO

Published in Nashville, Tennessee, by Thomas Nelson. Thomas Nelson is a registered trademark of Thomas Nelson, Inc.

Published in association with KLO Publishing Service, LLC (www. KLOPublishing.com).

Thomas Nelson, Inc., titles may be purchased in bulk for educational, business, fund-raising, or sales promotional use. For information, please e-mail SpecialMarkets@ThomasNelson.com.

Scripture quotations marked MSG are from *The Message* by Eugene H. Peterson. © 1993, 1994, 1995, 1996, 2000. Used by permission of NavPress Publishing Group. All rights reserved.

Scripture quotations marked NASB are from NEW AMERICAN STANDARD BIBLE˚, © The Lockman Foundation 1960, 1962, 1963, 1968, 1971, 1972, 1973, 1975, 1977, 1995. Used by permission.

Scripture quotations marked NIV are from HOLY BIBLE: NEW INTERNATIONAL VERSION˚. © 1973, 1978, 1984 by International Bible Society. Used by permission of Zondervan Publishing House. All rights reserved.

Scripture quotations marked NKJV are from THE NEW KING JAMES VERSION. © 1982 by Thomas Nelson, Inc. Used by permission. All rights reserved.

Library of Congress Cataloging-in-Publication Data

ISBN 978-1-59555-096-5

Printed in the United States of America

10 11 12 13 14 RRD 9 8 7 6 5 4 3 2 1

In loving memory of
Rachel Brooke Litton
(1977–2004)

Contents

Author's Note

The beloved novel *To Kill a Mockingbird* has been quoted throughout *The Mockingbird Parables*. Because many versions of the book are in print—and to avoid a long list of end notes—the chapter in which a passage appears is indicated after the quoted material.

You do not have to have read *To Kill a Mockingbird* to enjoy, understand, and grasp the transformative power of these parables. This book is not intended to be an academic study of Harper Lee's masterpiece. Instead, it's a collection of parables that delivers the wisdom found in the urgently relevant themes of *To Kill a Mockingbird*—in a way that illuminates our faith and highlights what it means to truly love our neighbors. It is my sincerest hope that the ideas discussed in the pages that follow will capture your imagination, disarm you, move your spirit, allow God to speak to you, change you, and inspire you to head out to the used book store, dust off an old copy of *To Kill a Mockingbird*, and open it for yourself. But until then, I will make sure you are equipped with all you need to embark on this journey with me.

Parable Reflections, located at the end of the book, is a collection of questions meant to motivate further thought and, perhaps, incite you to action.

To Kill a Mockingbird
and the Power of Parables

*The destiny of the world is determined
less by the battles that are lost and won
than by the stories it loves and believes in.*

—HAROLD C. GODDARD (1878–1950),
FROM *THE MEANING OF SHAKESPEARE, VOLUME 2*

*Our vocation is not to give visibility
to our powers but to God's compassion.*

—HENRI NOUWEN (1932–1996), FROM
COMPASSION: A REFLECTION ON THE CHRISTIAN LIFE

T he opening lines of the novel are so familiar now, but I can still remember the first time they were read to me:

When he was nearly thirteen, my brother Jem got his arm badly broken at the elbow . . .

It seems that I was nearly thirteen myself, huddled uncomfortably in the backseat of the family station wagon with my brother and sister, listening intently as the sun burned down on the windshield mural of red clay, bright chrome bumpers, and the green exit signs of that big American highway careening by.

When it healed, and Jem's fears of never being able to play football were assuaged . . .

The three of us leaned toward the front passenger seat, crowded and awkward, like turtles stretching our necks, straining to hear over the rhythmic drone of rubber sailing on the hot Georgia asphalt . . .

It began the summer Dill came to us, when Dill first gave us the idea of making Boo Radley come out . . .

Our mother, an English teacher, delivered the beautiful compilation of Americana and grace that is *To Kill a Mockingbird* with splendid drama and nuance, as if the car were her classroom that long vacation drive to the beach.

And as is the case with all of the finest novels, every character seemed familiar, every street seemed a real street, every building like someplace I had seen before. Although there was much I did not understand about the story on that first read, every word seemed authentic, palpable, and deeply affecting. I was moved by the courage of the protagonists, stunned by the childlike honesty of Scout Finch, horrified by the evil hidden in the hearts of even the good churchgoing folks, and devastated by the injustice done to Tom Robinson. Although I could never have articulated it at the time, I was introduced to both the beauty and the sickness that resides in the heart of humanity. It was genuine, candid, and so truly an American story. Only with maturity did I begin to appreciate the power of the novel's delicate blend of nostalgia and humor, conveyed with such charm and subtlety that I couldn't help but be disarmed. Only then, with all my defenses down, did I realize that I was being gently forced to look in a mirror to examine my own life and community, and unequivocally take note of the beauty, the blemishes—and the pressing need for change.

In the many years since that vacation, I have turned to the pages of *To Kill a Mockingbird* countless times, often still hearing my mother's voice and feeling like that thirteen-year-old kid, watching the windows full of huge clouds surfing over the heat and busyness of the southern highways. Yet with each visit to Maycomb, Alabama, I find there is more exploration needed, more to the characters I thought I knew. Like thirty million other readers, I've fallen in love with the novel, and for many years have made an annual summer pilgrimage to Maycomb through the pages of Harper Lee's classic, each time finding something fresh and remarkable.

It is a unique novel because of its continued relevance to readers. At the time of the book's publication in 1960 (and the subsequent release of the Academy Award–winning movie), it rattled the establishment with its forthright and severe criticism of racism, and doubtless opened the eyes of average Americans, pushing the nation toward true civil rights for all its citizens. In fact, I believe it stands today, revered and often quoted, as a beacon pointing the way toward our continued pursuit for equality in the world. The novel has been described simply as the story of one man's stand for racial justice, but we cannot ignore the many other valuable themes and lessons found in its pages.

As witness to its continued importance, the British and American Librarian Societies voted *To Kill a Mockingbird* as the one novel everyone should read before they die; it seems to remain perpetually enshrined at the top of the lists of most-discussed novels on numerous literary Web sites. The story's role as a staple in the education of millions of school-age children across the world also cannot be underestimated. It is the nation's most widely read novel in grades nine through twelve. It is a piece of literature that stands animate in its interminable relevance, and is a book I can truly say I will never grow tired of reading.

Whenever I find myself reflecting on its significance, I am always struck with wonder at the legend that Harper Lee became so frustrated with writing *To Kill a Mockingbird* that she simply tossed the entire manuscript out of her New York City apartment window . . . where it could have been lost forever down sewer grates, under the feet of passersby, blown to the windshields of fleeting cabs. But as the story is told, an encouraging phone call from an editor just moments later from an editor sent her to the sidewalk to recover the abandoned work.

I have always taught my students that the best novels will allow us to look at life through different-colored lenses, to observe the world from different perspectives. I begin by asking them to imagine putting on a pair of glasses when they open a work of literature. I endeavor to help them understand they will bring their own shades and perspectives to the reading, and that the colors of those lenses will affect the way they interpret the meanings of stories. I often think of the scene from the movie *Dead Poets Society*, in which master instructor John Keating has his students come to the front of the room to stand on his desk and see the classroom from a different vantage point, announcing, "I stand upon my desk to remind myself that we must constantly look at things in a different way."[1] I tell my students that through life experiences, friendships, education, and maturity, their worldview will continue to change.

And yet while they will always bring their own perspective to the literature we study, I tell them they should also be willing to try to observe the world through the author's eyes. Reading is a partnership between reader and writer; readers are always participants in the story on some level. An easy example that comes to mind involves a wonderful poem by e. e. cummings titled "i carry your heart with me." The poem will certainly represent something completely different to someone who has been married for thirty years than it might to a newlywed couple. Or think about John 3:16 (NIV) for a moment: "For God so loved the world that he gave his one and only Son . . ." Those words evoke a much deeper and personal meaning to me now that I am a father than they did when I was merely a college student. Consider how much heavier those words might fall on the ears of a father or mother who has experienced the loss of a child.

So it is with my own perspective that I offer these parables drawn from a book I love so well. Swiss theologian Karl Barth's writing first pointed me toward the truth that there is an aliveness to the Scripture, that we are not to simply read the biblical narrative, but to experience it. Bernhard Anderson elaborates on this concept when he suggests that we "read it [the Bible] as a story that is not just about other people of long ago but that is about us in the places where we are living."[2] I have always approached *To Kill a Mockingbird* (and many other novels) in this same way, wearing lenses of faith, and so my reading of the novel has always been a spiritual one. It is very important to understand, especially for those who will critique this work, that it is not my intent to speak for Harper Lee. Rather, through this collection of stories, I want to share with you how powerfully *To Kill a Mockingbird*'s moral and spiritual lessons have spoken to me.

My interpretation of the book has changed through the seasons of my life. During college, I was inspired by Lee's main character, Atticus, a steadfast, uncompromising hero of whom another character says, "We're so rarely called on to be Christians, but when we are we have men like Atticus to go for us" (22). I was mesmerized by his courage and eloquence, and I focused mainly on his heroism and compassion, understanding it as a call to make a difference in the world. It was the trailhead of a path that would lead me into education, and eventually into writing.

Later I studied theology, and I began to notice a distinct difference in the way the *Mockingbird* heroes and heroines conducted themselves; you could say I was impressed at what Lee's protagonists *didn't* do. In a world that celebrates power, in which to be heard you need the loudest voice, and where the most forceful affirmations are generally considered "right," these special characters challenged me with their adherence to a different set of rules and beliefs. But in Maycomb, the truth was told by children, and justice and courage were disciplines practiced not with guns, legislation, or propaganda, but by characters who peacefully and courageously denied themselves out of true compassion for others. I began to wonder if these characters operated cognizant of an alternative, more eternal reality—one far superior to the oppressive power systems under which they lived. These characters, with all their shortcomings, seemed to model the teachings and walk in the footsteps of faith. I developed a deep admiration and longing to practice this type of heroism in my own life.

As I began to read the novel through the lenses of fatherhood, I once again turned to Atticus Finch in awe of his patience and wisdom with his children. As a father of four, I often find myself asking how Atticus might handle the children if he were riding along with us on our eighteen-hour car ride to the beach. I often (unsuccessfully) try to place myself in his shoes. Forget parenting gurus like Dr. Spock or Dr. Dobson—Atticus Finch is my model for parenting.

One reading of the novel was particularly difficult for me. On a hectic evening in July several years ago, my wife and I received a dreadful phone call: my sister and her unborn child had suddenly passed away. Months later, I remember opening that old, worn mass-market copy of *Mockingbird* in the grief-induced haze of that heartbreaking loss, and the words sent tears streaming down my cheeks. You see, my little sister was very much our family's Scout Finch; she lived her life undeterred by other people's expectations of her. It is hard, sometimes, to read Scout's words without hearing my sister's voice and recalling how vibrantly, compassionately, and fearlessly she lived her life. I strive to live with the same type of passion.

My most recent explorations of the novel have been the most important, because I have come to perceive the spiritual significance *To Kill a Mockingbird* can hold for people of faith. Maybe it was Harper Lee's own words in her 1961 essay, in which she describes love as "manifestations of a power within us that must of necessity be called divine, for it is no invention of man,"[3] Maybe it was Atticus's explanation to his daughter, Scout, about why he had to take the Tom Robinson case: "Scout, I couldn't go to church or worship God if I didn't help that man" (10). Or quite possibly it was the eloquence of Eugene Peterson's admonitions about, "words that God's Spirit . . . uses to breathe life into our souls."[3] Over the past few years I have come to ascertain something very spiritual about the themes veiled in the pages of this deeply familiar American novel. There are messages scribed here so bent with common sense, compassion, and grace, truths so deeply founded in our conscience as Americans, that they simply cry out to be unfolded. In many ways, this book was born of Atticus Finch's celebrated pronouncement, "You'll never really understand a person . . . until you climb into his skin and walk around in it" (3). This decree for true compassion is the foundational message of the novel, and similarly an attribute that is a principal charge of faith. For it is *compassion* that is the origin of what was G. K. Chesterton articulated as the "furious love of God." It is with that message of compassion and understanding that I learned to "climb into the skin" of these folks from Maycomb, and discovered that they are deeply and unabashedly reflections of ourselves and our communities. It was with this new way of considering Lee's novel that I began to write *The Mockingbird Parables*, with hopes that together we could better understand how to live in our world—as better human beings, as better neighbors, and ultimately as active participants in the unfolding story of redemption. But what, exactly, are parables?

Parables are simply stories, and stories are not only a powerful way to deliver meaning—stories are the voice of humanity. Consider for just a moment how you might explain your day at work, or how you met your significant other, without the use of stories. We define and explain ourselves, our families, and our communities through stories.

It is an understatement to assert that the Christian faith tradition has a strong foundation in parable telling. The founder Himself taught us using parables, and nothing articulates the power of His storytelling like the Bible. In the gospel of Matthew, the disciples approached Jesus and asked Him, "Why do you tell stories?" or "Why do you speak in parables?" Jesus responded with some vigorous words about his teaching style: "Whenever someone has a ready heart for this, the insights and understandings flow freely. But if there is no readiness, any trace of receptivity soon disappears. That is why I tell stories [parables]: to create readiness, to nudge people toward receptive insight" (13:11, MSG). The disciples, like all good Hebrew boys of the day, would have been very aware of the Torah's prophecy about the power of Jesus' storytelling: "I will open my mouth and tell stories; I will bring out into the open things hidden since the world's first day" (Matt. 13:35, MSG). This teacher understood the power of a story and its deep influence over human beings.

Jesus' parables were not fairy tales or folk tales but rather realistic stories that took place in familiar settings of life. They invited His listeners to easily imagine themselves as participants. It is important to understand that Jesus was teaching people who were steeped in religious culture and "church talk." It was a culture in which every aspect of their lives was centered on religion. The young men of the Jewish tradition actually had entire books of the Torah memorized by the age of twelve. It is curious, then, that securely in the midst of His explanation to the most intimate of His followers about why He chose to teach in parables, Jesus quoted the prophet Isaiah, saying, "Your ears are open but you don't hear a thing. Your eyes are awake but you don't see a thing"

(Matt. 13:11, MSG). So what exactly was Jesus saying to them about these stories?

I vividly remember the day my dad's grandfather clock was delivered to our house, carried through our front door in a large box by two men from the furniture store. It was a beautiful, ornate clock that sat in the foyer on prominent display for everyone who entered our home to see and to admire. It seemed to tower over me, grand and austere, a beautifully crafted bronze clock face, a cherry wood exterior, and a large glass door that sheltered the pendulum and all the other fascinating machinery in constant *tick-tock*ing motion. I grew up with that clock, sleeping soundly, and I took little notice of it. It was simply a part of my landscape. I was never acutely aware of the grandfather clock's domineering presence in our home until I went away to college. But in my first visit home after being away for several months, I found myself lying awake in my room for miserable hours, covering my ears with pillows, turning on fans, doing anything to sleep through the constant ticking of the pendulum and worse—the ringing of each hour . . . 1:00 a.m. . . . 2:00 a.m. . . . It was like trying to sleep with Big Ben firing away in my brain. My friend Chet recounts a similar story about the time his father took over a new church in a small Kentucky town. The parsonage at the church sat directly next to a busy set of railroad tracks. It took the family months to learn to sleep there, but once they did, he remembers they barely took notice of the large freight trains roaring by in the middle of the night. The rhythmic, disjointed clamor of cars passing over wood and iron, even the horn of the engine began to come and go completely unnoticed by his family. Chet jokes that his father placed the guest room at the front of the house to ensure they never had company for too many nights.

I believe this might be the point Jesus was making to His followers when He quoted the prophet. I personally find it is easy to become so accustomed to, and comfortable with, religious language that I start to sleep easily through the night, not hearing the words and messages that should keep me awake and vigilant. You see, there are themes and messages in *To Kill a Mockingbird* that have sounded off like the hours of a grandfather clock, waking me like the blaring horn of a freight train, allowing me to hear parts of the gospel to which I had become deaf . . .

Not that a novel can supplant the story of God, but peering into the courtroom experience with Atticus, watching carefully what happens at the oak tree with Jem and Scout, or sitting with the ladies at the Maycomb missionary tea may provide fresh words and a new perspective to enhance what it means to live a life of faith; as Jesus says, to hear in new ways what has been "hidden since the foundation of the world." You see, faith, by its very nature, is sustained, transformed, and maintained by stories . . .

Despite the technological revolution, social efforts by the nations of the world, advances in medicine, and the digital connectedness of modern life, our world still seems to be fraught with a deepening sense of anxiety, despair, and isolation. You don't need to leave your neighborhood these days to find broken people in desperate need of help and healing. Where have Christians been in all of this?

Somewhere along our journey we have managed to reduce the power of the good news of Jesus to a system of delivery, one that will carry us to the "sweet by and by." We have managed to relegate Jesus' command to love your neighbor as yourself to the periphery of our faith practice. It is a dilemma that Harper Lee articulates so profoundly through the words of Miss Maudie: "There are just some kind of men who—who're so busy worrying about the next world they've never learned to live in this one, and you can look down the street and see the results" (5). The philosopher Dallas Willard describes this phenomenon in his distinguished work *The Divine Conspiracy*. He implies that we are living in a religious culture in which our primary concern has become to know "whether or not one was going to 'make the final cut.'"[5]

One might speculate that we have condensed the gospel to the weight and size of a train ticket; our primary goal is to have the conductor punch the card as we piously sit back to watch the broken world pass by outside the window. In doing so, we have ignored the truth found in the command of love from John in chapter 3, verse 16 (For God so loved the world . . .). We have forgotten that our primary call is to bring reconciliation to the world—the whole world. C. S. Lewis writes so brilliantly in *The Weight of Glory*, "It may be possible for each to think too much of his own potential glory hereafter; it is hardly possible for him to think too often or too deeply about that of his neighbour."[6] And yet that is what many of us have become comfortable with in the twenty-first century. We have ignored our neighbors. We have forgotten the words of Jesus: "I was hungry and you fed me, I was thirsty and you gave me a drink, I was homeless and you gave me a room, I was shiver-ing and you gave me clothes, I was sick and you stopped to visit, I was in prison and you came to me" (Matt. 25:34, MSG).

You and I—neighbors, Christians—we are the only vehicle for God's reconciliation of the world. There is no back-up plan. I hope these parables will help you rediscover what it means to be a good neighbor—and to experience the gospel message retold in modern language, unobscured by religious dogma. It is my hope that these parables may, in some small measure, play the role of a grandfather clock in the foyer of your faith. I am inviting you to take part in the story, in anticipation that it might aid you, as it has me, in imagining the possibilities and the hope of the gospel, ques-tioning what it really means to be a person of faith in our world.

The Parable of Boo Radley: Discovering Our Divine Mysterious Neighbor

What comes into our minds when we think about God is the most important thing about us.

—A. W. TOZER (1897–1963), FROM *THE KNOWLEDGE OF THE HOLY*

I would rather live in a world where my life is surrounded by mystery than live in a world so small that my mind could comprehend it.

—HARRY EMERSON FOSDICK (1878–1969), AMERICAN CLERGYMAN

D ill Harris, a friend of the novel's narrator, Scout Finch, poses the question: "Wonder what he [Boo] does in there? . . . Looks like he'd just stick his head out the door" (1). Scout tells us in the opening lines of *To Kill a Mockingbird* that the entire drama began to unfold, according to her older brother Jem, "when Dill first gave us the idea of making Boo Radley come out" (1).

Boo Radley is a mystery. He is described as a phantom who remains curiously locked away inside his home. While the children play in plain view of the Radley house, they are captured by the ambiguity and folklore of Boo. Jem describes legends of his unseen neighbor with whimsical and child-like fervor: "he dined on raw squirrels and any cats he could catch, that's why his hands were bloodstained . . . what teeth he had were yellow and rotten . . . and he drooled most of the time" (1). The question of Boo Radley, posed by the children, is the grand enigma of *To Kill a Mockingbird*. It is the splendid canvas on which all the other profound conflicts in the novel are painted; it is the vigor that ensnares our imagination, and the constant tension edging us forward as the drama unfolds. "Who is Boo Radley?" may be one of the most haunting questions in the history of American literature.

Every magnificent story, every grand adventure, every worthy quest, is initiated by a question. Questions lead us, stir us forward, unsettle us from our comfortable chairs, and send us off into a greater story. I find questions are the origin of many meaningful relationships and ventures, and the mystery of Boo reminds me of my first auspicious adventure. One of my earliest childhood recollections is of a dimly lit, dark-stained, creaky wooden stair-well, each foreboding and shallow step adorned with black vinyl footpads that led the narrow path to a mysterious lone room on the top floor of my grandparents' aged row house. My siblings and I would dare each other to make that climb; each step filled our hearts with anticipation and anxiety until our fear of the unknown simply wouldn't allow us to go up any further toward the door. My grandfather occasionally observed our game and enjoyed height-ening the drama. He would often remark, "I'm not sure what is in that room, I haven't been up there in years." The question that enthralled my imagination and pushed me off exploring centered on what was behind that door.

It is not just true that journeys begin with a question—rela-tionships do as well. I was in college when I was captured by another mystery. I remember the tree line glistening with the fail-ing rays of sunlight, framing the shadowed red bricks of the dorm building with a soft glow. The pocket of cool green lawn in the front exhaled the colors of fall, and as I edged across the parking lot toward the entrance I noticed a girl sitting on the sidewalk. Her brown hair was pulled back through a baseball hat, her T-shirt draped casually with a red flannel shirt. I thought she was beauti-ful. My inquisitiveness about the girl enchanted me in that moment, and that moment has unfolded into ten wonderful years of mar-riage. It was the beginning of a much greater story.

In the novel, the crucial inquest is: "Who *is* Boo Radley?" The question certainly attracts my students to the narrative. When I teach *To Kill a Mockingbird*, I ask my high-school scholars to sketch what Boo Radley might look like—to explore the mystery of Boo. It is an exercise I have grown to love. The representations range from hilarious to grotesque; students arrive with pictures of a fearsome character, a sympathetic character, or something curiously in-between. It is enlightening to see how each student's imagination opens in a unique way when he considers the inexplicable Boo. I have often wondered what their drawings might look like if I could ask them to complete the same project in response to a more profound question: "Who is God?"

Who is God? We may call it the Great Question, but it is unequivocally the fundamental question of life. Our response to it is the very foundation of the way we live out our lives, shaping and defining our every endeavor, relationship, and action. It is the principle guiding just how our short time here on earth will look. Just as my students quickly recognize that *To Kill a Mockingbird* is built on a question, we approach God emphatically recognizing that our faith is also founded upon a question.

In a world full of technological interconnectedness, with googled explanations at our fingertips, it is difficult to embrace the concept that the Great Question is pivotal to our faith. However, with a child securely in his lap, Jesus pointed out, "I tell you the truth, unless you change and become like little children, you will never enter the kingdom of heaven" (Matt. 18:3, NIV). Too often we misuse this verse to validate the conventions of a blind or unquestioning faith, but Jesus is intending to communicate something quite different by focusing our attention on the attributes of children. (As my wife and I can easily affirm, you only need to spend several minutes in a house full of kids to realize that questions are their primary mode of communication.) Jesus wanted us to recognize that children are driven by questions.

The more I scrutinize the pages of the Bible, the more I understand that questioning is central to the Christian tradition. Abraham and Sarah, Job, Solomon, King David in the Psalms, the disciples, Paul . . . all were voracious questioners. In fact, the biblical narrative implies that the "Who is God?" question is the very axis of our faith until the time when "the mystery of God will be accomplished, just as he announced to his servants the prophets" (Rev. 10:7, NIV). "Who is Boo Radley?" eloquently mirrors the question that underlies our very existence, that should ignite our imaginations and stir us with passion on our spiritual journeys. The persistence with which we ask this question defines the vitality of our faith in God.

Dangerous Dares and Fishing Poles: Protecting the Curiosity to Seek God

The novel never really offers a clear explanation or depiction of Boo Radley. Scout describes Boo as a shut-in, a phantom, a mysterious character that she has never seen emerge from his run-down house: "People said he went out at night when the moon was down . . . Any stealthy small crimes in Maycomb were his work" (1). Scout, Jem, and Dill, are spellbound with the question, and it is their persistence that ultimately drives Boo into their lives. Asking the question always leads to the process of seeking answers.

Their first act of *seeking* comes in the form of a dare when Dill goads Jem to touch the Radley house, a challenge born by the children's notion that Boo might just come out of the house to chase after them when he sees them in his yard. Jem, the oldest of the three children, takes him up on it. He charges through the Radley yard as fast as he can run, touches the house, and sprints fearfully back past Dill and Scout—all the way to the Finch house without even pausing to look back. The three even act out plays about Boo based on the folklore of the town's adults—an entertaining process that reminds me of what we try to do in church sometimes. They attempt to contact him again one evening under the cover of dark, sneaking through the Radley garden with a fishing pole to deliver a message to his window. The truth of Boo Radley is the one treasured inquiry the children trail throughout the novel; it reflects the very nature of how we seek to know God.

The children provide a wonderful model of how we should pursue God. Unfortunately, we fear language that involves too much questioning, seeming especially haunted by the mystery of God. Call it pursuing he Great Question, call it curiosity, the children are simply *seeking* to know the real Boo Radley.

A marvelous undertaking began with the riddle of what was behind that locked door at my grandparents' house—and it eventually allowed us a glimpse into our mother's childhood, when we overcame our fears enough to pursue the truth. Similarly, a wonderful connection began when I pursued my question about the girl that auspicious fall evening in college. My initial question led to curiosity, and no matter how long we have been married, I am still intently seeking to know more about the lovely mother of my children. As Jesus pointed out in Matthew 7:7-8 (NIV), "Ask and it will be given to you; seek and you will find; knock and the door will be opened to you. For everyone who asks receives; he who seeks finds; and to him who knocks, the door will be opened."

The children's act of seeking Boo Radley represents the quintessence of what it means to be the people of faith. In Genesis 32, Jacob actually wrestled with God through the night, and at daybreak God told him, "Your name is no longer Jacob. From now on it is Israel (God-Wrestler)" (v. 28, MSG). God's name for His people literally means *God Wrestler*—and like the faithful, Scout, Jem, and Dill are constantly grappling for answers about Boo that reach beyond the shallow explanations of the detached and impartial town elders.

Dining on Raw Squirrels and Cats:
The Dangers of Domesticating God

Some of the adults in Maycomb are a stark contrast to the three children in the way they approach the Radley question. We learn from the narrator that the Radley family is different from the rest of Maycomb in that they do not feel obligated to fulfill the religious traditions or common social practices of the time: "The Radleys, welcome anywhere in town, kept to themselves, a predilection unforgiveable in Maycomb" (1). The Radleys are unexplainable. The adults of Maycomb (much as we behave with God) either cannot accept or have grown too busy, too preoccupied, or too disinterested to pursue the "Who is Boo Radley?" question. They have chosen instead to define him, ignore him, and keep him in his place. To believe in God does not mean that we rest on a definition. Or as Anne Lamott articulates, "The opposite of faith is not doubt, it is certainty."[1]

In the story of creation, Adam was given power to name all of the earth's living creatures; thus it was assumed in the ancient world that when you named something, you then had power over it. This concept is one of the earliest signs that the God of the Hebrews, the God of our Bible, was much different from gods of the competing cultures. The very name He provides—I AM—implies that He is larger than being named and will not be controlled. Jesus, whose name means *I AM saves*, also speaks to this freedom and elusiveness in His conversation with Nicodemus in John 3:7 (MSG), "You know well enough how the wind blows this way and that. You hear it rustling through the trees, but you have no idea where it comes from or where it's headed next. That's the way it is with everyone 'born from above' by the wind of God, the Spirit of God." The contrast between the children and the adults of Maycomb is not meant to elevate doubt to some iconic goal or noble idea. The children *know* Boo is there, but are still *seeking*, and it is their inquisitiveness that drives them toward relationship with him. It is the wrestling or, more clearly articulated, the *seeking* that defines a vigorous and burning faith.

Seeking is an indispensable component of relationship. Think for a moment about the meaningful relationships in your own life, and you will find that each reflects a desire to continue the process of curiosity, in search of know more about the other. Since seeking is so crucial, then, why is it our nature to define God rather than to engage Him each day with curiosity? Even Moses was compelled to define God by asking the Almighty to show His face; yet God responded, "I will cause all my goodness to pass in front of you, and I will proclaim my name, the LORD, in your presence. I will have mercy on whom I will have mercy, and I will have compassion on whom I will have compassion . . . you cannot see my face, for no one may see me and live . . . There is a place near me where you may stand on a rock. When my glory passes by, I will put you in a cleft in the rock and cover you with my hand until I have passed by. Then I will remove my hand and you will see my back; but my face must not be seen" (Ex. 33:19–23, NIV). Moses can know God's goodness and His glory, but may not see His face. The mystery of God is one that will not be revealed.

We say that God is good and that He died for our sins, but how can we really know this unless we continue searching out the questions and seeking Him to engage with us in the conversation about who He is? It sounds scary to have no control over God, just as it is daunting for the adults of Maycomb to engage a mysterious and unknown Boo Radley. Our vision of God should always be dynamic; it is relational and therefore always evolving. When we begin to define what God can and can't do, we stop allowing Him to shape us. The first time He doesn't respond the

23

way we just know He should, our definition of Him is invalidated and sometimes our faith is broken. When we stop living in the tension of the "Who is God?" question, we begin to formulate a God who is beholden to our transient rules, doctrines, expectations, legalities, and regulations. The result is a petty, unforgiving God, exalted not by seekers but by those who wish to define Him so they may go about their business unbothered. A God like this might even resemble the terrifying Boo of the childrens' imaginations: "Once the town was terrorized by a series of morbid nocturnal events: people's chickens and household pets were found mutilated; although the culprit was Crazy Addie . . . people still looked at the Radley Place, unwilling to discard their initial suspicions" (1). We must, like the children of *To Kill a Mockingbird*, continue seeking God as the central expression of our faith. Fortunately for us, we aren't the only party pursuing the relationship.

A Knothole in the Oak Tree: God is Always Pursuing Us

Early in the novel, Scout is walking past the edge of the Radley yard when her attention is captured by something in a tree. She investigates; there is something hidden in a knothole just within her sight. It seems to be tinfoil, but when Scout reaches in, she is pleasantly surprised to find a couple pieces of chewing gum. The gift giver is, of course, Boo Radley. Scout tells her brother about the surprise, and on their next visit to the tree they are overjoyed to discover a small box of antique coins placed in the knothole. Jem is immediately mesmerized with the Indian-head pennies. Boo Radley is pursuing a relationship with the children, much as God has been chasing after us since . . . well, since the beginning of time. Early in Genesis, we learn God visited Adam and Eve. "When they heard the sound of GOD strolling in the garden in the evening breeze . . . GOD called to the man: Where are you?" (Gen 3:8–9, MSG). God knows Adam is there; He is calling out to him for relationship, just as Boo Radley is reaching out to the children.

Jem and Scout continue to receive gifts from Boo in the knothole of the tree. This beautiful sequence in the novel reflects the manner in which God pursues relationship with us. Boo offers gifts that fit in the everydayness of the children's lives, and places them where they will see them—meeting them where they are. The tree is a landmark they pass by every single day on their way home from school, a part of their daily monotony and routine.

I am finding that God works the same way. When we take the time to observe the day a little more like children, with a little more inquisitiveness, we begin to see the gifts that God leaves for us in the midst of our routines. God has positioned gifts in the knotholes along the way of my journey in so many distinctive ways: a deer running in front of me on an afternoon walk, a dove flying alongside me on a bike ride, the silence of the Andes mountains in Peru, or a simple but beautiful moment with my family.

The knotholes are present at eye-level in each of our daily lives; it is up to us to take the time to catch the glint from the tinfoil. "Long before we first heard of Christ . . . he had his eye on us, had designs on us" (Eph. 1:11, MSG).

Another significant intimation in this sequence of Boo's gift giving is the actual nature of his gifts. It is evident that Boo knows the children (as God knows us). He is aware of what brings them joy, and what secures their imagination. And as we start to pay attention to the gifts God leaves us, we also learn more about Him. Boo's gifts to the children begin with simple pleasures—like sticks of gum and lucky pennies—but as the story goes on, the gifts become more personal: Scout finds two delicately crafted but familiar images carved out of soap. She tells us, "One was the figure of a boy; the other wore a crude dress" (7). The gifts continue to appear, and the next week the children discover a tarnished medal hidden in the tree. In the carefully crafted soap figures we find that the gift giver knows the children. They quickly recognize that the carvings are made in their own images. The tarnished medal left at the tree turns out to be an award from a long-ago Maycomb County Spelling Bee, a prize that provides further clues to the nature and the character of the gift-giver. God's gifts to us, like Boo's gifts to the children, often reflect both His knowledge of us and truths about His nature. After all, it is not a stretch for us to imagine a God who would use a tree to deliver us into relationship with Him. As Boo's actions so clearly suggest, He is a God who pursues us.

Laughter, Blankets, and Sewn-Up Jeans:
God is Always Present with Us

Although Boo Radley isn't visible to the children (for most of the novel), he maintains an active presence throughout the story. He seems to never be too far from them, an ever-present observer. Early in the novel, Scout climbs into a tire and is pushed by Jem and Dill. The tire rolls out of control down the street and right into the gates of the dreaded Radley house. As Scout recounts the experience she tells us just underneath the sound of her brother yelling, and the chaos of being spun around and around inside the tire, "I had heard another sound, so low I could not have heard it from the sidewalk. Someone inside the house was laughing" (4). This is the first clue in *To Kill a Mockingbird* that Boo is watching the children. Such vigilant oversight is hard for us to grasp when it comes to God, and I imagine that close observation of our behavior must have to elicit laughter from the Almighty on some (well, with me at least, *many* occasions. I wonder if we might take ourselves less seriously, somehow, if we expend a little more time contemplating what might amuse God in our day-to-day activities; it is peculiar to me that so many people seem offended by the idea that the God of the universe has a healthy sense of humor.

Boo's vigilance over the children is reiterated when Jem and Dill decide that they should sneak up to the Radley house under the cover of night and place a note for Boo in the window. The result is disastrous! Mr. Radley, Boo's older brother and apparent caretaker, comes out of the house and fires his shotgun into the air, the kids frantically run for their lives, and in the chaos, Jem's pants are caught in the barbed wire fence around the Radley's garden. In his haste to escape, Jem leaves his "breeches" tangled in the fence and goes charging across the neighborhood pants-less. Later that night, Jem sneaks out of the house to retrieve what was left behind. What he finds unsettles him so much that it takes him several days to tell Scout. "When I went back . . . they were folded across the fence . . . like they were expectin' me . . . And something else'—Jem's voice was flat . . . 'They'd been sewed up.'" Jem continues ruminating on the reality that someone knew he was going to come back for the pants. "Can't anybody tell what I'm going to do lest they know me" (7).

The children are traversing precarious ground by sneaking to the house in the dark and are clearly disobeying their father, Atticus, in the process. Boo Radley doesn't intervene when his older brother comes out of the house and shoots his gun. Certainly, the presence of the gun implies danger to the children, and although they are unharmed, it is not because of Boo (in this particular situation)—an observation that will become more relevant. It can be difficult for us to wonder why God intervenes at times to keep us from harm, and at others, like Boo, stays indoors. I recall the tragic death of my younger sister; our frantic, passionate prayers for God to intervene seemed to fall on deaf ears that dreadful day. God, without explanation, appeared to stay in the confines of His house, choosing not to intervene—at least not in any way we could recognize at that moment.

There is also much of God's grace reflected in Boo Radley's act of repairing Jem's pants and folding them over the fence—*after* the disastrous event. God always seems to be there to sew together areas of my life that have been ripped apart, and although the seams might show, and the hems might not be perfect, it is clearly His handiwork that holds me together. It is fascinating to consider that God knows the decisions we will make, the tragedies we will endure, and seems to formulate His entrance along the way—in His own time. Boo knew Jem would sneak back for the torn-up pants, after disobeying his father and almost getting injured. He places the sewn-up breeches on the fence so that Jem doesn't have to venture into danger again.

When a winter fire breaks out at their neighbor's house and threatens the entire neighborhood, Jem and Scout find themselves standing in the cold street watching the town attempt to rescue Ms. Maudie's possessions from the inferno. During the fire, someone wraps the oblivious Scout in a warm wool blanket. The children are dumbfounded with amazement when their father tells them Boo Radley did it. To this stunning revelation, Jem responds, "Just think Scout . . . if you'd just turned around, you'da seen him" (8). It is so often true that in the tragedies and tough times of life we rarely notice until later how God was present with us, placing the blanket around our shoulders, keeping us from the cold. Like the writer of Joshua proclaims, "the LORD your God will be with you wherever you go" (1:9, NIV); our God is attentively watching over us . . . just as Boo is present and vigilant with the children.

Kitchen Knives and Front Porch Windows:
God Still Intervenes in the World

One of the major conflicts of the novel is resolved in the final chapters when the drunken Bob Ewell, a malicious person who beats his own daughter and is responsible for the death of an innocent man, threatens the lives of the children. He attacks them at night as they walk home from a Halloween pageant. The mysterious Boo Radley hears the cries of the children, finally emerges from his home, and rushes to save them from the drunken assailant. Atticus understands the depth of Boo's heroism, and with plainspoken sincerity he pauses momentarily in front of the unlikely hero on his way back into the house to check on his injured son and says, "Thank you for my children, Arthur"" (30). It is at this moment of crisis that Boo Radley chooses to emerge from his home. He moves from the imaginations of the kids to reality very quickly at a critical moment.

For many of us who have experienced real-world tragedy and have asked, "Where was God?" this might be the most difficult connection to make. There is no clue as to why Boo Radley chooses to act in this scene, just as there was no clear reason that God did not intervene in my sister's tragic death. There are plenty of scriptures that speak to the mysteriousness of God's timing and purpose. In Ecclesiastes, the writer tells us, ".there will be a time for every activity, a time for every deed" (3:17, NIV). Out of frustration and confusion toward God's apparent inaction Job says, "What strength do I have, that I should still hope?" (6:11,

NIV). It is a deeply personal struggle to face the apparent absence of God's intervention in these times.

We might receive an answer to that question at the very end of the novel, as we follow Scout Finch and Boo Radley walking hand-in-hand to the door of his home. As she stands at Boo's front porch, she notices that his view of the neighborhood is completely different from any she has seen. She realizes that from the Radley front porch, Boo has a clear view of the "entire neighborhood"— not just one house. Every place the children frequent—from Miss Maudie's yard to their own front porch—is in sight of Boo's window. It provides a sobering reminder to us that God's perspective on our lives is eternal and infinitely broader than our own.

From the Radley porch, Scout understands not only that Boo's view of the world is much different than her own, but that he has been vigilantly watching over "his children" for seasons, "Summertime and his children played in the front yard . . . Fall and his children trotted to and fro around the corner . . . They stopped at an oak tree, delighted, puzzled . . . Winter, and his children shivered at the front gate, silhouetted against a blazing house . . . Summer, and he watched his children's heart break. Autumn again, and Boo's children needed him" (31). Scout makes it clear in the passage that Boo has been present with them through every season of the novel. Boo is the representation of a God who is not only present, but one who intervenes directly into our world.

In the third chapter of Exodus, God tells Moses, "I have taken a good, long look at the affliction of my people in Egypt.

I've heard their cries for deliverance from their slave masters; I know all about their pain. And now I have come down to help them" (v. 7, MSG). And maybe, much like God in this passage, it is the cries of *his children* that Boo Radley hears from his front porch window, "'Run, Scout! Run! Run!' Jem screamed . . . 'Jem, Jem, help me, Jem!'" (28). Boo grabs a kitchen knife and runs directly into the fray. It appears a much different action than leaving gifts in the oak tree, mending jeans, or placing a blanket around Scout's shoulders. Boo is directly and physically affecting the outcome of events; it is difficult for many of us to recognize that God operates in this way too.

When faced with the sobering question of whether God still performs miracles, or directly intervenes to change the course of events, I often wonder if our perspective is all wrong. I consider this with great trepidation; our family has experienced our share of bitter tragedy, and sometimes just turning on the evening news is enough for me to lament that God could tolerate such pervasive calamity and heartache in our world. But what if from God's eternal perspective the gifts left in the knothole of the oak tree are as important as saving the children from Bob Ewell's drunken assault? What if the healing of the cancer patient and attracting the attention of a child with a passing butterfly are of equal importance in moving people toward relationship with God? We only know the outcomes in our world; we cannot see our lives from God's perspective. If we choose to acknowledge His pursuit of us, then we must also admit that He performs miracles in our world—and with no expectation of return.

Soap Dolls, a Broken Watch, and Lucky Pennies: God Is Our Good Neighbor

Scout tells us in the closing chapter of the novel, "Boo was our neighbor. He gave us two soap dolls, a broken watch and chain, a pair of good luck pennies, and our lives . . . We never put back into the tree what we took out of it" (31). Boo Radley provides us with a beautiful representation of the nature of God. Giving is truly the essence of our divine neighbor. As Scout recounts the gifts Boo has given the children, it reminds us of the marvelous heredity of giving bestowed on us from our God that is to be passed on to our neighbors. When we endeavor to throw off the conventions of religious inertia and approach the Great Question with the same curiosity that the children of the novel pursue Boo Radley, I am confident we will discover in amazement a God who is actually pursuing us. We will begin a magnificent journey of restoration and relationship with our Creator that will change our hearts and send us reaching out to the world. When we seek and pursue Him, we will find He is a good neighbor who embraces our inquisitiveness and blesses our curiosity, is present with us, and intervenes in our lives. We will find a God, much like Boo Radley, who will surprise us with the joy of a gift that is more intimate than soap dolls and good-luck coins. This divine neighbor fills our earthly lives with mystery and wonder and promises of more.

The Parable of House Fires
and Church Collections:
Our Responsibility to Care
for the Neighborhood

*The Bible tells us to love our neighbors, and also to love our
enemies; probably because they are generally the same people.*

—G. K. CHESTERTON (1874–1936), ENGLISH AUTHOR AND PHILOSOPHER

*Let everyone sweep in front of his own front door,
and the whole world will be clean.*

—JOHANN WOLFGANG VON GOETHE (1749–1832),
 GERMAN WRITER AND POLYMATH

The narrator of our story, Scout Finch, describes the Radley family as peculiar because they never open their home to others or visit with their neighbors on Sunday. "The shutters and the doors of the Radley house were closed on Sundays, another thing alien to Maycomb's ways" (1). Once upon a time in America, it was a Sunday afternoon custom to open your front doors and spend time with friends, family, and neighbors. I think back with great fondness about the community in West Virginia where my parents began their life together. While the cultural tradition of Sunday visitations was fading into the hectic pace of modernity in the mid-Seventies, my parents were deeply attached to a faith community during that time and spent many Sunday lunches gathered around the kitchens and living rooms of friends. I once confused the deep feelings of belonging that I had as a child there with nostalgia, but as an adult I have realized there was something truly unique about the practices of the people of faith that surrounded our young family. I was only about Scout's age, but clearly remember a sense of security, knowing our lives were so closely intertwined with our church and our neighborhood. We were fortunate to be part of a church that was devoted to caring for its immediate neighbors. I recollect afternoons riding on errands with my "Uncle" Freddie in his pickup truck over worn tire paths that led through lush green aisles of his orchard into an expansive front yard ornamented with large black kettles full of steaming apples. Our entire congregation was there, working to make apple butter to be canned and sold to alleviate the various needs of families in our town. The church felt an ownership toward the problems in its neighborhood. It left a strong impression on me as a child; the church approached caring for the community with the consternation of the apostles in Acts 6:3, who deemed it so important that they appointed specific leaders of the church who were "full of the Spirit and wisdom" (NIV) to carry out the task.

There was a unique richness to the life of our faith community as a result of this devotion, and it was reflected in my parents' relationships. I recall my amusement at the laughter and good-natured quarrelling of my parents and their friends from church gathered around a card game that involved hysterical yelling and ringing of a bell that rested in the middle of our antique kitchen table. The faithfulness to neighbors was even borne out in the weekly routines of our street. I can't forget playing in the front yard of our house and observing a yard or two away my dad's tall, stern silhouette in the twilight as the neighbors convened with waving hands and exasperated expressions to catch up on the latest news. That lasting image of my father always reminds me of Atticus Finch, Scout and Jem's father, gathering to talk with the other adult neighbors on the main residential street in Maycomb. To this day, I can't read *To Kill a Mockingbird* and not visualize the Finch's street as my own in West Virginia. It was one long line of homes surrounded by farms on both sides; gardens, gravel driveways, split-rail fences, honeysuckle blooming, and wild blackberries that edged the slow road for our enjoyment on evening walks. Mom and Dad eventually moved away from that town to pursue new careers and bigger dreams, and although they made terrific friends around the country in that process, I am not sure that they ever really encountered community quite like they did in there at the small Methodist church. There was something substantial happening in that village that I long for even now. It was a whole community working together toward restoration, a sense of connectedness founded not in similar interests, but in a passionate mission to serve the neighborhood. In many ways, I see comparable commitments revealed in the stories of Maycomb, Alabama.

Maybe it is the prevalence of upward mobility, the hectic pace of modern life, or the result of ever invasive consumerism, but it seems that many of the pastors I speak with today deplore their churches' unwillingness to commit time and resources to their immediate neighbors. I recall a recent visit to a local church during which the pastor pointed despairingly to the single parents and struggling families in his own congregation whose needs were continuing to go unmet. The problem goes beyond our churches; in fact, it transpires rather too close to home. Many of you will lament with me about our culture's idea of togetherness, which once meant congregating in each other's presence on front porches across the neighborhood, but has been reduced to congenial waves across paved streets and well-manicured lawns at the open and close of automatic garage doors. You might say we have left behind something very essential to America, but for people of faith, it is a more dire circumstance. In the second chapter of Acts, the words of Luke elucidate just how far we have fallen away from our commitment to our neighbors: "All the believers were together and had everything in common. Selling their possessions and goods, they gave to anyone as he had need" (vv. 44–45, NIV). Our churches have become uncomfortably like the Radley house, with its closed shutters, locked doors, and apparent indifference to the suffering of our neighbors. While it must be plainly stated that Maycomb, Alabama, as a community is one with major warts (racism being the most egregious), there are also instances—borne out by the heroes of the story—that demonstrate something very essential about the responsibility we have to serve our immediate neighborhoods. Through these characters, we can hear again what it means to be people who love and care for one another, we can stop viewing faith as its own disconnected vocation, and start practicing it responsibly as an integral part of the life of our very street, our own neighborhood, our hometown.

The Best Cakes in Maycomb: Offering Our Talents to Our Neighbors

Scout, Jem, and Dill soon discover something wonderful about their neighbor, Miss Maudie: "She made the best cakes in the neighborhood" (5). At the beginning of the novel as the children play outside during the summer, their neighbor and family friend, Miss Maudie, opens the door to relationship by baking for them. While it is probably true that the fastest way to a child's heart is through his stomach, there is something much deeper and more spiritual occurring in this sequence. A new trust is being forged and an essential friendship nourished, as the children spend time eating cake on Maudie's front porch. The celebration of relationship over food has been a staple in accounts of the biblical narrative from Genesis through the Last Supper of the Gospels, but the significance of Maudie's offering is found when Scout tells us Maudie was the best cake maker in the neighborhood. Miss Maudie is doing something very holy by offering the children her God-given talent. I love the way Paul explains this in his first letter to the Corinthians, as he talks about gifts from God. He says, "God's various gifts are handed out everywhere; but they all originated in God's Spirit . . . Each person is given something to do that shows who God is: Everyone gets in on it, everyone benefits" (12:4–7, MSG). We often overspiritualize gifts and talents, only to view them in the context of traditional church functions, but gifts and talents include our abilities and interests, and if Paul were to write today, he would speak of lawyers and accountants, writers and athletes who honor God in the way they carry out the skills He has given them. When we dedicate our talent to serving a neighbor, it is possibly one of the highest forms of worship; something sacred transpires when we sacrifice our time and dedicate our God-given loves and talents to one another.

A close friend of mine, Mike, shared an extraordinary story with me several summers ago. His church was attempting to find a way to serve their neighbors. They tested a Web site on which the people in his church community could connect their passions, talents, and skills to those in need. Plumbers, electricians, schoolteachers, and headhunters volunteered several hours a week to fix broken sinks, replace faulty wiring, tutor struggling students, and write résumés. Mike said the response was overwhelming, and we wondered over breakfast what it would look like for every church to engage the needs of their immediate neighborhoods with that type of fervor.

Sitting in Silence on the Front Porch: The Power of Offering Our Presence to Others

Maudie intentionally gives her talents, but she also offers her presence, a gift instrumental in fashioning a deep friendship with Scout (and earning the right to be her mentor). "Miss Maudie and I would sit silently on her porch, watching the sky go from yellow to pink as the sun went down" (5). I am always taken back at this scene, with its understated depiction of the value of just being there, of just being present in the moment with someone.

Mother Teresa once commented that "God is the friend of silence." It is clear that Maudie is contented sitting silent with Scout, simply satisfied spending time with her. I often find offering my presence to neighbors much more arduous than offering my talents. (Sometimes it is more convenient to mow a neighbor's lawn than to sit with him, isn't it?) While no words are spoken between Maudie and Scout, it is obvious that there is an exchange happening; it is spiritual and much more substantial than words. And through the comfort of sitting together, Scout comes to know she is a priority to Miss Maudie. We are so regularly tempted to say the right words; we feel pressure to always have the correct answer. Yet God comes to us in silence, a still small voice . . . not always with answers to our questions; sometimes only with His divine presence.

A friend I spoke with recently about the power of presence recounted her tragic story of having contracted a dreadful flu during pregnancy and losing her baby as a result. Her church community reached out to her with volumes of commentary about her misfortune. Although few actually stopped by, explanations ranging from "It was God's will" to "It was just nature's way" poured in; every e-mail, card, letter, or phone call would end with some variation of "Please let me know if I there is anything I can do to help." She remarked that she will never forget when the newest neighbor from her street appeared at the door one afternoon with dinner slung over her arm in bags. As my friend greeted her, the neighbor began by saying, "This is really some kind of hell, isn't it?" My friend recounted how powerful it was that this neighbor stopped by and sat with her at times, commiserating in silence.

There are volumes of books about our deep need as human beings to be in the company of others. I wonder if the greatest thing we can offer a neighbor is our mere presence. It could be more powerful than any word we might ever utter. I am sure this willing silence, this attendance to our fellow man, is what is meant in this quote attributed to St. Francis of Assisi: "Preach the gospel at all times and when necessary use words."

Having Walter Over for lunch:
There Should Be No Strangers
in God's Neighborhood

Jem stops Scout from beating up her classmate, Walter Cunningham, in the school yard. "'He didn't have any lunch,' I said, and explained my involvement in Walter's dietary affairs." At this point Walter has recovered, but stands defensively eyeing Scout, wary of another attack. "'Your daddy Mr. Walter Cunningham from Old Sarum?' [Jem] asked, and Walter nodded" (3). In this scene, Scout has once again found herself in trouble with her first grade teacher when she is asked to explain why Walter has no lunch. She blames Walter for her troubles and is busy exacting revenge on the poor lunch-less boy when Jem stops her. It doesn't take Jem long to understand the problem and offer a solution. Scout tells us that Jem breaks out into a smile, and says, "Come on home to dinner with us, Walter." (3).

I love how effortlessly Jem recognizes what is happening and invites Walter over for dinner. At first glance there are so many Biblical themes we could glean from this simple invitation. We could discuss the Hebrew culture of hospitality toward strangers; we could focus on the ease with which Jem identifies and responds to Walter's need, or maybe even his joy in extending the invitation to Walter. Jem extends his invitation with absolute confidence; this attitude has obviously been modeled for him. He shows no inclination to check with Atticus (his father), and there isn't the slightest hesitation that Calpurnia (the housekeeper) will mind. Jem knows that his house is open to strangers, and there is nothing more beautiful than that kind of home.

I don't remember that my brother, sister or I ever really had to ask our parents to have someone over. In fact, by the time I was away at college, I think my sister had friends permanently camping out at our house. I was fortunate to grow up in a home where the door was open to anyone. I wonder how often we realize, when we gather to worship, that the very purpose of the church community is the same.

It is evident in this scene also that Jem really doesn't view Walter as a stranger. God has never predetermined who can come over for dinner—it is an invitation open to every human being. We are invited in to eat at the Lord's table no matter who we are, what we have done, where we come from. God has invited us in; how much more should we make it a priority to do the same for others, to model God's gracious invitation? Jesus makes this clear in His mission statement (the Sermon on the Mount) when He says, "Keep open house; be generous with your lives. By opening up to others, you'll prompt people to open up with God, this generous Father in heaven" (Matt. 5:14, MSG). And again in Matthew 22, He describes His kingdom as a wedding banquet for which "the servants went out on the streets and rounded up everyone they laid eyes on, good and bad, regardless. And so the banquet was on—every place filled" (v. 8, MSG). Jem's invitation to Walter is one founded in complete confidence that there are no strangers in his father's house.

Drowning His Dinner in Syrup:
Respecting the Differences of Others

When Walter arrives at the Finch house for lunch and sits down to eat, he offers up a strange request to Atticus. Scout describes the scene as Walter interrupts their dinner to ask for syrup: "he poured syrup on his vegetables and meat with a generous hand. He would probably have poured it into his milk glass had I not asked what the sam hill he was doing" (3). Scout is outraged by Walter's behavior because it is completely foreign to her. Scout's insensitivity offends her dinner guest, and Calpurnia quickly pulls Scout into the kitchen to reprimand her: "'There's some folks who don't eat like us,' she whispered fiercely, 'but you ain't called on to contradict them when they don't. That boy's yo comp'ny and if he wants to eat up the table cloth you let him, you hear?'" In the face of Calpurnia's fury, Scout makes it clear that she doesn't consider Walter her guest—instead, she views him as different because he is part of the poor *Cunningham* family.

I love when the cultures of different families collide over dinner. We have had some amusing experiences with our own extended family at holiday gatherings. Through marriages, deaths, and remarriages, we come together with different backgrounds, experiences, traditions—and have learned how to compromise. There have been some tensions along the way, always followed closely by laughter. Serious matters have had to be addressed, such as who eats last, who prays (when and how), the seating arrangements . . . We even have an ongoing pizza topping debate.

Somehow we manage beautifully. Notice the wisdom of Calpurnia in this scene; it reminds me of First Corinthians: "I have a serious concern to bring up with you, my friends, using the authority of Jesus, our Master. I'll put it as urgently as I can: You must get along with each other. You must learn to be considerate of one another, cultivating a life in common" (1:10, MSG). I always consider the analogy of my own family when I read this scene, and it makes me wonder if God doesn't feel like giving us Calpurnia's speech when he looks at all our denominations. I wonder how many souls miss out on the invitation to dine with God while Baptists, Methodists, Lutherans, and Catholics remain disconnected from one another because of our mild divergences. In my hometown, there are at least ten different denominations represented; they rarely work together to accomplish anything. As Scout points out when she acknowledges that she doesn't see Walter as her guest, the origin of our problems with others begins with our intolerance and sanctimony toward their differences.

The Meanest Old Woman in Maycomb: So Who Exactly Are Our Neighbors?

Midway through the novel, we are introduced to the cantankerous Mrs. Dubose. Jem and Scout must pass by her house each day on their way to town. Mrs. Dubose always greets them with taunting and insults: "Don't you say hey to me, you ugly girl!"

She harasses the children with vile accusations and hateful commentary about their father and the rest of the Finch family.

Mrs. Dubose behaves as hostilely as any character in the book, and yet I am reminded that it is even the most loathsome of characters in our lives that we are called to love: "I'm telling you to love your enemies. Let them bring out the best in you, not the worst. When someone gives you a hard time, respond with the energies of prayer" (Matt. 5:44, MSG).

What happens next in the story is perfectly framed against these words of Jesus. Jem loses his cool and goes flying into her yard to destroy her flowers in retribution. He doesn't calm down until he has annihilated every one of Mrs. Dubose's prized camellia bushes. How many times have you wanted to respond to someone like this? Everyone knows a Mrs. Dubose. But Jesus calls us to love the people who resemble her. I have been in circumstances where I felt accosted, and in the deepest recesses of my gut strained not to retaliate with expletives and insults (and you know, occasionally I have failed; and sometimes even when I have managed a closed mouth, the response in my heart was equally as dreadful). Love my enemies? There is a deep-seated truth in this scene that goes far beyond our response to the hostility of others.

As punishment for destroying her bushes, Jem goes each day after school (for weeks on end) to sit by Mrs. Dubose's bedside and read to her (Scout accompanies him). Each visit lasts a little longer, and the children must endure her constant barrage of terrible insults; however, they faithfully attend to her until finally the day arrives when Mrs. Dubose curtly informs them, with no indication of gratefulness, that they will not have to return to her home. It is only several days later we find the truth behind Mrs. Dubose's misery: "Mrs. Dubose was a morphine addict . . . she took it as a pain killer for years. The doctor put her on it . . . Jem, when you're as sick as she was, it's all right to take anything to make it easier, but it wasn't all right for her'" (11). And so we uncover the hidden explanation for Mrs. Dubose's misery. After her death, Atticus even describes her as a model of true courage because of her resolve in the face of illness and addiction; she achieves her aspiration to die free of her morphine addiction.

It is in Atticus's wisdom that we are able to see past the disease and pain that made her a terror to the children. It is often true that we are completely unaware of difficulties veiled in the lives of our own Mrs. Duboses. My desire is that the next time we are being cursed by someone in the next lane of traffic, slandered by a coworker, or insulted by a parishioner of our congregation, we remember Mrs. Dubose—it would serve us well. It is frequently not our neighbors themselves, but the sum of their shrouded afflictions that make them seem unpleasant.

Pitching in to Fight Fires:
Our Responsibility to Be There for the Crisis

Atticus wakes Jem and Scout at one o'clock in the morning when a dreadful fire has broken out at Miss Maudie's house. "We stood watching the street fill with men and cars while fire silently devoured Miss Maudie's house" (8). The children look on as the fire threatens the entire street. Every man in Maycomb has apparently emerged from the safety of his own home to fight the fire and try to rescue Maudie's furniture from the flames. I marvel at the way Maycomb responds to the crisis: it is all hands on deck; everyone pitches in. Even those whose homes are not threatened quickly appear to rescue as much of the furniture as they can while Miss Maudie's and Mr. Avery's houses burn. This response to the fire is an impressive example of our responsibility to be there for various "fires" in our immediate neighborhoods.

We have been fortunate to take part in some vital service recently at my own church. The fire in our town is an economic downturn. Our church has responded in a meaningful way. A group of us, led by our executive pastor, have worked in unison to create a community resource center to combat the fallout of a bad economy. We spent a summer cleaning up some old mobile classrooms, scrubbing walls, cleaning carpets, and gathering furniture. We prepared an area that would allow us to expand our food bank, create a clothes closet with winter coats for families in need, and a work space equipped with a day care, computers, printers, and volunteers to assist those currently needing to find jobs. The most humbling part of that process was how enthusiastic the children were about helping out—it reminded me of the importance of teaching them to serve others. Many families contributed to the project, and I was able to witness firsthand the powerful bonding experience of working together and knowing that we would be meeting the needs of our neighbors.

I have also visited magnificent church buildings—I mean absolute, architectural beauties—situated in the middle of struggling communities. Some friends have told me of a ten million–dollar building that contentedly rests surrounded on all sides by government housing and hurting people. The parishioners of this church, including the pastor, drive in on Sundays from affluent neighborhoods in luxury vehicles and promptly scatter after the service. We wondered if they would so comfortably travel in and out of that neighborhood if the metaphorical fires were real—smoking on the streets all around their building. I am convinced that if we are to bring restoration to the world, redemption that began with the resurrection to these people, it must begin, as in Maycomb, with all hands on deck, caring for our own street. I can only imagine how the neighborhood mentioned above could be radically transformed if the resources, talents, and love gathered in that expensive sanctuary were unleashed into the surrounding community.

The firefighters of Maycomb take me back to that St. Luke's Church community in West Virginia, to that entire congregation sacrificing their Sunday afternoons to care for people in need. When we ignore the fires burning in our own neighborhoods, we reduce our churches to expensive country clubs and the gospel becomes nothing more than meaningless propaganda. I pray we can learn to fight, to put out the neighborhood fires, with the same industriousness as the men of Maycomb.

Taking Up Collection: Supporting Those in Need

The events that transpire when Calpurnia takes the children to her church constitute what is undeniably one of the most moving scenes of the novel. It happens at the African-American community called the First Purchase Church, the church attended by Helen Robinson, Tom Robinson's wife. Tom is the black man who has been falsely accused of raping Mayella Ewell, and as he sits in prison awaiting trial, his wife and children are struggling to get by. At the end of the service, the pastor of First Purchase, Reverend Sykes, closes his sermon and calls for an offering. The entire congregation comes forward one at a time to place coins in a coffee can at the front of the church. Scout and Jem provide their offering as well.

No matter how many times I read the novel, it is the following lines that always bring me to tears as this pastor empties the can in front of the congregation and begins to count the money: "'This is not enough, we must have ten dollars.' The congregation stirred. 'You all know what it is for—Helen can't leave those children to work while Tom's in jail. If everybody gives one more dime, we'll have it—' Reverend Sykes waved his hand and called to someone in the back of the church. 'Alec, shut the doors. Nobody leaves here till we have ten dollars'" (12). I can honestly say I have never witnessed this in a church service, never heard of it happening, and can't even imagine it taking place in real life, but there is something so moving about the pastoral determination of the reverend. "'Carlow Richardson, I haven't seen you up this aisle yet.' A thin man in khaki pants came up the aisle and deposited a coin . . . Reverend Sykes then said, 'I want all of you with no children to make a sacrifice and give one more dime a piece . . .' Slowly, painfully, the ten dollars was collected. The door was opened, and a gust of warm air revived us" (12). How could you read this scene and not think that we need more pastors like Reverend Sykes of First Purchase Church? You can almost feel the discomfort of the closed door, the sweating, the heat of the room, the smell of perfume, the rhythm of people fanning themselves to stay cool, and Reverend Sykes's eyes raking over each parishioner as he scans the sanctuary, determined to make sure that Helen Robinson can feed her family that week.

Isn't this the way church should work? Not a soul openly questions the reverend's authority in this scene. They are set on caring for one another. This was the way the early church operated in caring for its own community: "And so it turned out that not a person among them was needy. Those who owned fields or houses sold them and brought the price of the sale to the apostles and made an offering of it. The apostles then distributed it according to each person's need" (Acts 4:34–35, MSG).

Part of the dilemma in the modern church's lack of impact on culture originates with the fact that at times we are inept at even caring for our own congregation. How much more appealing would the gospel message be if we took care of our own church members like this? Our institutions have become bureaucratic, our denominations large, our mortgage payments obese, and more often than not, very little of the tithe goes to help the local community. When the haves are unwilling to meet the basic needs of the have-nots, the message of salvation is drowned out. Rob Bell and Don Golden make a great point in their latest book, *Jesus Wants to Save Christians*, when they consider that maybe God doesn't care what we eat or what we own as long as the basic needs of the people around us are being met.

Find out from your church exactly where your money goes. Check out the Advent Conspiracy online. Skip out on an extravagant Christmas and help someone with his mortgage. Cut back on vacation and buy gift cards so a struggling family can afford school clothes. Look around your church community and imagine that Reverend Sykes has closed the sanctuary doors; he is counting the offering and his eyes are on you to take care of each other.

Helping Out Mayella Ewell and Saving Jem and Scout: The Call To Be a Neighbor Is Dangerous

One lesson that cannot be overlooked in this parable is that fulfilling God's call to love your neighbor—our call as the church to be there for the immediate community—can be very dangerous work. I think God blesses our faithfulness to each other, but the reward isn't always what we envision. One of the greatest examples of acting out of compassion for a neighbor in *To Kill a Mockingbird* is portrayed in the character of Tom Robinson. Tom is on his way home from work when he walks by Mayella Ewell's run-down house, and he faithfully responds to her call for help.

His compassion places him in peril, as Tom later explains to the prosecuting attorney that each time he passed by her house she seemed to have something she needed help with: "'choppin' kindlin', totin' water for her. She watered them red flowers every day . . . I was glad to do it, Mr. Ewell didn't seem to help her none, and neither did the chillum" (19). Tom has made a habit of being neighborly to the lonely and abused daughter of Bob Ewell, and this compassion eventually costs him his life.

Another example of the danger of following Christ's call to become a neighbor takes place in a scene at the end of the book, when the mysterious Boo Radley comes out from his home to rescue the children from certain harm at the hands of Bob Ewell. I can only imagine Boo's discomfort, emerging from his house in this scene after spending most of his life (and the entire story) in hiding. But he is driven out by the need of the children: Boo sees Bob Ewell trying to squeeze a knife through Scout's costume . . . then suddenly Ewell finds himself violently pulled backwards and thrown to the ground.

Boo's commitment to the children becomes a costly life-and-death struggle, which is the same for us when we grasp the essence of what it means to be a part of the community of Christ. Jesus calls us to "pick up our cross"—to carry an instrument of execution. He preached a message to "love your neighbor as you love yourself" and ended up nailed to a tree. The apostle Paul wanted to go before Caesar as a witness to the resurrection of Jesus and his journey led to a shipwreck, arrests, beatings, and eventually public execution. There is a cost involved in loving our neighbor that we cannot ignore, yet it is the essence of the Christian faith—it is the surrender of self that leads to community.

Walking in Someone Else's Skin: Caring For Your Neighbor Begins With Compassion

To Kill a Mockingbird is a story with a profound message about the significance of compassion. There is a deep-rooted, viable, and overflowing sense of connectedness that rises up from the seeds of genuine compassion. When true compassion grows roots in the fertile soil of our faith, it blooms in lush growth as authentic and satisfying as the honeysuckle and wild blackberries I remember so vibrantly decorating the path on my evening jaunts with Mom and Dad down our road in West Virginia. We must be careful not to lose the true meaning of community by eulogizing it as an ideal or a dream. It is an oft-cited quote from Dietrich Bonhoeffer that reminds us, "Those who love their dream of a Christian community more than the Christian community itself become destroyers of that Christian community even though their personal intentions may be ever so honest, earnest, and sacrificial."[1]

As reflected in my musings about the relational connectedness of my life as a child in West Virginia, real community begins with the concerted sweat and muscle of working for our neighbors, of rooting through the dirt, the differences, and the malignant illnesses of confinement that separate us from one another. This growth of responsibility to our neighborhood and of participation in the story of redemption begins with authentic compassion. Nothing reflects this commitment better than the lines of Atticus to Scout in the early pages of *To Kill a Mockingbird*: "You never really understand a person until you consider things from his point of view . . . until you climb into his skin and walk around in it" (3). It must never be lost on us that our God, in His effort to reclaim creation, saw fit to do the same, to climb into human skin . . . and walk around with us.

The Parable of Scout Finch:
The Role of Women in Faith

Men are taught to apologize for their weaknesses,
women for their strengths.

—LOIS WYSE (1926–2007), AMERICAN ADVERTISING EXECUTIVE
AND AUTHOR

No person is your friend who demands your silence,
or denies your right to grow.

—ALICE WALKER (B. 1944), AMERICAN AUTHOR
AND PULITZER PRIZE WINNER

J ean Louise Finch sits quietly listening in the bathroom, heart-
broken, threatened by the disapproval in her aunt's voice as
she berates Scout's father, Atticus, about his misguided practices in bringing up his young daughter. It takes a moment for Scout
to realize who they are talking about: "My heart sank: me. I felt the
starched walls of a pink cotton penitentiary closing in on me, and
for the second time in my life I thought of running away" (14).
Aunt Alexandra represents just one of the many forces in this
young lady's life that seem intolerant of her uniqueness. Jean
Louise, the narrator of the novel, goes by the name Scout. A *girl* . . .
named Scout? It is a name that reached out and grabbed hold of my
curiosity the first time I heard it. This little girl captured all of my
beliefs about the world—with her distinctive voice and personal-
ity—and, quite frankly, shook them up a bit. I remember the first
time I read the novel; I was immediately taken back by her character: A *girl* . . . named Scout? She exhibited the inquisitiveness,
strength, and ferocity that rivaled any of the boys I knew.

And Scout was a little more than just a character in the pages of
a book for me. I *knew* a Scout Finch; her name was Rachel. She
lived in my house and flourished with grace in the conditions of
family culture that occur naturally with having two older brothers.
My sister wore dresses and played with dolls, but as we grew older,
I noticed how her independence drew the constant displeasure of
those who deemed some of her interests too boyish. She could go
from a pretend tea party to the heated intensity of a backyard army
battle with uncanny ease. Basketball was a second religion in our
home, and she had a way of playing the sport that made opposing

coaches wish they had outfitted their players in football gear. Her take-no-prisoners approach to the sport was only rivaled by the care with which she applied her makeup before the game. Many adults were uncomfortable with her free spirit and her aversion to conform to their gender expectations. I watched as many in positions of power leveled disapproval toward her independence—simply because she was a girl. They were troubled by my sister because she didn't completely measure up to their ideas of what a girl should be.

Scout tells us that her brother and Dill spent their days playing together, "calling me only when they needed a third party. But I kept aloof from their more foolhardy schemes for a while . . . on pain of being called a girl" (5). It is early in the novel when Scout begins to bemoan being relegated to third-wheel status by the boys in her life. I always smile at Scout's clever delivery of the line, "on pain of being called a girl," because it vividly reminds me of Rachel. She was so often called on only when my brother and I deemed a supporting character necessary to play what were (in our minds) minor roles like Princess Leia to Han and Luke, Daisy to the Duke brothers, or the damsel in distress to our valiant knights. I remember one particular backyard reenactment of *Star Wars* when she finally put her foot down and informed my brother and me that one of *us* would function as the trio's Princess Leia for the time being. Much like the character of Scout, my sister demonstrated an unwillingness to walk tranquilly in line with what church and culture was conditioning the three of us to believe about the roles required of a girl. The position of women is one of the major social issues addressed in *To Kill a Mockingbird*, and it hinges on the daring Scout Finch's relentless engagement of the question: What does it truly mean to be a lady?

Maycomb is uneasy with this little six-year-old named Scout. Her reference to the penitentiary is a fear of being overwhelmed by the disapproval of her society; it is a lament that she will be somehow imprisoned by their expectations of how she should dress, act, and talk, simply because she is female. The starched-pink-cotton penitentiary is still in operation today. It is the unexplainable urge we possess to define each other's roles as wholly masculine or wholly feminine. It is the separate set of cultural, religious, and even political expectations of women. My sister's independent spirit railed against these unbiblical traditions. Although our narrator's spirit might be temporarily wounded by overhearing Aunt Alexandra's displeasure, she is Scout Finch; it is not in her nature to run from a fight.

Somewhere along the journey we have marginalized the truth found in the story of creation: that it is not just men, but also women who are created in the image of God. The book of Genesis tells us, "God spoke: 'Let us make human beings in our image, make them reflecting our nature'" (1:26, MSG). All human beings, both male and female, reflect characteristics of the Trinitarian God who created us. Many of us recoil from the idea of God's feminine qualities and yet our narrative is full of them. In Isaiah, God says, "As a mother comforts her child, so I will comfort you" (66:13, NIV). Even Jesus defies our gender roles, embodying characteristics that we deem feminine through His tenderness and compassion for people. If we truly are *all* reflections of God, we are gravely mistaken in identifying these divine qualities as gender-specific.

Maybe when we discourage women from exhibiting the qualities we deem as wholly masculine, we really aren't being honest with ourselves about the true nature of God. Our faith is filled with women who defied society's roles for them. From the oldest recorded poem in Scripture declaring God's work in the world, to the earliest witnesses of the resurrection of Jesus, the role of women is essential to the biblical narrative.

More Like a Girl Every Day:
Determination and Strength Isn't Just for Guys

"'Scout, I'm telling you for the last time, shut your trap or go home—I declare you're getting more like a girl every day.' With that I had no option but to join them" (6). I have always enjoyed this exchange between Scout and Jem as they are contemplating an invasion into the frightful Radley yard. Jean Louise Finch is just beginning school, and yet she is already cognizant of her inner resolve. We meet her early in the story as a child relatively unaware of the oppressive gender expectations of her culture. She displays a beautiful determination and strength unfettered by the teachings of her church and community.

We have decided that these qualities are masculine, and even today are subtly intolerant of the women who display them. Consider, for a moment, the public reaction to female politicians and leaders who personify these qualities. Consider the language we use to classify women who display the strength and determination of Scout. Yet women exemplifying this strength play a vital part in our story. From Miriam, Moses's sister, who is referred to as a prophetess and leader in the Exodus, to Deborah's role in Judges, strength and determination are both essential qualities for women of faith. This resolve is divine and is often played out more clearly in the actions of women. Don't agree with me? Try doubting a woman; try doubting God.

I will never forget our family vacation to Michigan. My brother and I were preteens at the time, and my sister was around Scout's age. I can recall our slow footsteps under clear blue skies and a faint sound of lapping waves resonating in our ears over the mounds of sand. The three of us crested the top of one impressive sand dune to look down and see that it dropped significantly to the beach and Lake Michigan. I remember my brother and I began to tumble down the steep incline toward the water, issuing a challenge to my sister. "You will never make it back up the dune," we taunted her. It was all she needed; she raced ahead of us toward the bottom and, much to my parent's irritation, refused all help as she slowly climbed her way back up. She would not be deterred; she would not be told no. And indeed, born naturally into the young Scout Finch, we find this sense of divine fortitude; she will not be excluded from the plot to discover Boo Radley, or any of her older brother's adventures. Scout mirrors the strength of biblical characters like Miriam, who kept watch over her baby brother Moses in the Nile, ignoring the orders of the Pharaoh that all Hebrew baby boys would be killed. It is the same steadfastness that led Mary, the mother of Jesus, to heroically suffer through the social scorn of being a pregnant and unwed mother at the request of her heavenly Father; and it is the same resolve that leads thousands of heroic women today in their quest to help bring God's vision of restoration to the world. Scout teaches us of what can happen when that divine strength and determination is allowed to grow in the heart of femininity.

Fistfights, Backyard Brawls, and a Ferocious and Nurturing Spirit

"Catching Walter Cunningham in the school yard gave me some pleasure, but when I was rubbing his nose in the dirt Jem told me to stop" (3). Scout's physicality makes me laugh when I read this scene, because my little sister was the same way. She would never be denied a position in the neighborhood football game. Early in Scout's story she catches poor Walter Cunningham in the school yard and lets him have it for his role in her awkward beginnings with the first-grade teacher, Miss Caroline Fisher. What a terror Scout must have been to poor Walter, who was truly innocent and probably unsuspecting of Scout's irritation with him, and yet she charges out to settle up with him for his "offense." She is not afraid to settle conflicts with her fists. Scout is a true tomboy with a spirit so strong that it often leads her soul-first into places she must not be; however, in most cases, she fights in defense of her loved ones.

Scout casts off society's gender definitions and displays the beautiful characteristics of God through this combination of fierceness and nurture. It is this impulse to protect those closest to her that, I believe, is another reflection of God demonstrated through the character of Scout. She possesses a warrior spirit that we have determined to be male, along with the nurturing spirit that we call wholly feminine. But Scout is just being herself.

These opportunities abound as the children begin to feel the invective of the town regarding their father's defense of the innocent Tom Robinson. It happens in the school yard where her loved ones are insulted and Scout is more than ready to fight: "'You can just take that back, boy!' This order given by me to Cecil Jacobs was the beginning of a rather thin time for Jem and me." (9). Again, at a Christmas visit to her Aunt Alexandra's house when Scout's spoiled cousin Francis begins to taunt her by insulting her father, Scout wastes no words on Francis. "This time I split my knuckle to the bone on his front teeth. My left impaired, I sailed in with my right" (9).

There is a ferocious instinct to be nurturing exhibited in some women that directly mirrors God's love for us. It is such a powerful impulse that it can often be witnessed in nature. One of my preferred paths to make my daily jog has several ponds that sit adjacent to the running trail. I am always fascinated as I run down the trail in the summer months to see how the mother ducks, meandering with their offspring along the water's edge, quickly spot me yards away, herd their ducklings safely into the pond, and then turn to keep a vigilant and wary eye in my direction as I pass.

This reflection of God's character in humanity is not only demonstrated by mothers. I recollect one of the few occasions when a heated football contest in our yard turned ugly. I don't remember exactly whether it was a late hit or a disputed pass-interference, but tempers flared and an elementary school–age rendition of a *West Side Story* brawl broke out. As the exchanges of words and shoves escalated, my brother and I were severely outnumbered in the dispute and began to circle the wagons. Before any adult could intervene, we were engaged in a free-for-all with several of the neighborhood boys. It seemed to go on uninterrupted forever; I am sure, in retrospect, it was only seconds. But I will never forget the face and the cries of the unfortunate fourth-grade boy who realized he had been tackled and was being viciously punched by my little first-grade sister who had charged into the fray. From the time she was able to talk, she referred to my brother and I as "her boys," and she would not be denied an occasion to defend us.

We also see Scout's nurturing qualities with Jem. She shows a patience with him early in the novel, even as he excludes her from his and Dill's boyish schemes: "Jem told me I was being a girl, that girls always imagined things, that's why other people hated them so, and if I started behaving like one I could just go off and find some to play with" (5). She never really holds these exclusions against her older brother and remains deeply engaged in his life.

Scout's capacity for nurturing is especially clear at the end of the novel, demonstrated in the way she instinctively tends to the needs of the reclusive Boo Radley at her home. First she leads him to a secluded and shadowed chair on the porch farthest from her father and Mr. Tate where she understands he will feel most comfortable; at the end of the novel she gently takes Boo's arm and allows him to walk her down the street to the front porch of his home.

This quality of Scout's spirit reminds me of the Old Testament story of Esther. It is Esther's protective spirit that compels her to find favor with the Persian king Ahasuerus and to rescue her people from certain destruction. These qualities are reflections of God, and it is certain that without them and the women who held fast to them, many of the great turning points in God's redemption of mankind could not have been accomplished. As writer John and Stasi Eldredge comment so succinctly about women, "When the history of the world is finally told rightly . . . it will be clear as day that women have been essential to every great move of God upon this earth."[1] But society is uneasy with the women who violate their conventions and exhibit these divine qualities, and Scout soon feels the tyrannical influence of their apprehension.

Small Stoves, Tea Sets, a Ray of Sunshine, and Oppressive Expectations

As the novel evolves, Scout comes face-to-face with the intolerance of what society defines as inappropriate for women, gender expectations that suffocate the uniqueness of her God-given qualities. The main voice of oppression comes, as it often does, from someone in the story who is part of the Finch clan. Scout explains her Aunt Alexandra's vision of femininity while attending the Christmas celebration; on top of her objections to never wearing a dress, "Aunt Alexandra's vision of my deportment involved playing with small stoves, tea sets, and wearing the Add-A-Pearl necklace that she gave me when I was born; furthermore, I should be a ray of sunshine in my father's lonely life. I suggested I could be a ray of sunshine in pants just as well" (9). Of course, these were requirements enforced by Southern tradition, and not too long after the women's suffrage movement. Today the language and the expectations are more refined, and the words conveyed in a more tolerant and politically correct way, but the theme of the message is delivered to young women just as clearly.

The neighborhood scold, Mrs. Dubose, who takes pleasure in screaming insults at the children from her front porch, also constantly questions Scout about why she wears overalls instead of a dress and camisole. The requirements of entrance into the world of women might sound a bit outdated, but they are, at their heart, the same as today's message to women. It is a call to conform, to submit, to be tempered, and to be defined by the dogma of culture and religion. Although different words are used now, our patriarchal society's discomfort with women's divine strengths is still very evident. Take a moment to consider the superlatives used to praise women, and what feminine qualities are exalted and valued in our modern culture. Most involve denying strength and holding fast to appearance, and as you go down the list, you will notice they are all very superficial. This is nothing new. I read recently that Eleanor Roosevelt, one of the strongest women in the history of American politics, was asked in an interview near the end of her life whether she had any regrets. Her response was heartbreaking. This woman who had dedicated herself to helping others responded that her only regret was that she had never been pretty. She had been harassed by others (including her own family) and all of her life called "granny" and "the ugly duckling." She was shamed by the media for her *appearance*. Rather than celebrating her strengths, Eleanor Roosevelt had been accosted by journalists and her family for the way she looked.

Scout faces taunting in this same vein much later in the novel. After Atticus has lost the Tom Robinson case, she attends a gathering of women and is chastised by Miss Stephanie Crawford for her unapproved appearance at court. "'Whatcha gonna be when you grow up, Jean Louise? A lawyer? . . . Why shoot, . . . you've already commenced going to court.' The ladies laughed again . . .'" (24). Stephanie finishes her rebuke of Scout's behavior by pointing out that she won't get very far in life until she learns to start wearing dresses. Scout confronts the message to which all women are subjected; it is a voice that communicates her appearance, and not her strength, is what legitimizes her in the world of women.

Scripture is wrought with a clear message of Jesus' utter disregard for appearance and social rank. In Judean society, it was a major taboo for a man to even speak to a woman who was not his own wife or daughter; yet Jesus interacted regularly with foreign women, He taught women, ignored ritual impurity laws, and readily accepted women into His inner circle of followers. As society continues to placate women, uncomfortable with their likeness to the Creator, why does the church not stand in the way?

Women Are Sin by Definition, and Missing Out on the Spirit and Context of the Bible

Women have played such a vital role in the Bible that it is hard to imagine Christianity has encouraged gender oppression . . . but sadly the church has done far more than simply promote these attitudes. Miss Maudie, Scout's neighbor, explains that the religious folks who pass by her backyard on the way to church believe that women are sin by mere definition. She says, "They take the Bible literally, you know" (5). Although many in the church are too sophisticated to voice their beliefs as inelegantly in today's twenty-first century culture, there are still thorns of this attitude protruding through the core doctrines of many denominations.

Let me pause for a moment to clarify. The Christian church is not at the top of the list of institutions and systems employed to subjugate women. However, it is the church's role to be at the forefront in the quest for true equality. It should be the church that leads culture toward affirming the divine strength of femininity! Whether our denomination espouses such dogmatic beliefs about the role of women or not, we are all at least guilty of complicit silence. Even today many believers pull the following individual verses out of context to define women's roles in their churches and in marriage. For example, Ephesians 5:22 says,

"Wives, submit to your husbands as to the Lord" (NIV). Another misused verse better reflects Miss Maudie's commentary: "Don't let women take over and tell the men what to do. They should study to be quiet and obedient along with everyone else. Adam was made first, then Eve; woman was deceived first—our pioneer in sin" (1 Tim. 2:11–14, MSG). It is, in my estimation, a combination of arrogance, an unwillingness to listen to God's spirit, and a refusal to recognize the clear biblical themes that must enable some churchgoers to read these verses as directives for women of faith.

Miss Maudie's proclamation about taking the Bible literally reminds me of Matthew 5:29. It says clearly, "If your right eye causes you to sin, gouge it out and throw it away" (NIV). I wonder if those who support the suppression of women under the guise of taking the Bible literally should be listening to the audio version of *The Mockingbird Parables* for lack of an eye or two. In order to use the Bible to suppress women, one must ignore the fact that Jesus' ministry was supported by women, and although He had twelve male followers, Luke strongly suggests that as many women traveled with Him and "were helping to support them [Jesus and the disciples] out of their own means" (Luke 8:3, NIV). Of course, Matthew 5:29 should be read in the context of the story. And there are very serious questions about the translation and context of the passage in Timothy. In fact, it is true that simply reading three verses beyond Ephesians 5:22 can help us gain a completely different understanding of Paul's meaning. He continues with a parallel command in Ephesians

5:25 (NIV), saying "Husbands, love your wives, just as Christ loved the church and *gave himself up for her*" (emphasis mine). He is not calling for women to submit to their husbands as one might glean from reading only one verse, but clearly articulates marriage as an equal partnership requiring the submission of both parties to each other.

Claiming women's sole responsibility for sin is another confused interpretation of the Scripture. The idea that women were wholly responsible for sin's entrance into the world is totally unfounded. (Genesis 3:6, Romans 5:12–21, and 1 Corinthians 15:21–22 all clarify that both male and female were complicit in the Fall.) Sadly, though, my friends who grew up in the evangelical world can recount hundreds of stories that reflect this terrible coercion. One particular Christian university would expel female students who were pregnant, not allowing them to finish their current coursework, but would allow their male partners to remain in school. There is actually a church community just a few miles from my home that requires the silence of women during community worship. I attended a wonderful presentation by author and speaker Phyllis Tickle, who told a heartbreaking story of a woman ostracized from her Southern church community for divorcing an abusive husband.

Scout is equally as skeptical about this view of women, saying, "My confidence in pulpit Gospel lessened at the vision of Miss Maudie stewing forever in various Prodestant hells" (5). The church's involvement in this is so shocking that at times I wonder if it is a tactic of the enemy to handicap the progress of our mission here on earth, to silence the feminine side of divinity that is so vital to the redemptive movement. But suppression continues to happen inside the halls of our churches, even when a much truer and more radical vision is spelled out by Paul in Galatians 3:28 (MSG): "In Christ's family there can be no division into Jew and non-Jew, slave and free, male and female. Among us you are all *equal*" (emphasis mine). This is a call that must be heard if the gospel's liberating freedom is to be recognized in the world. We cannot miss the characteristics of God expressed in our sisters of faith; if we do, we will miss much of the compassionate strength and fierce loyalty of God's character. We serve a God who sets out to free slaves, one who operates in complete opposition to the world's definition of power. The church should follow suit.

Miss Caroline Fisher's Class Spokeswoman: The Role of Women as Church Leaders

Early in the novel, in the first days of Scout's school experience, she emerges as both the class leader and a threat to Maycomb County's newest first-grade teacher. In fact, the other students begin to look to Scout as their spokesperson to explain to Miss Caroline Fisher the unique ways of Maycomb life and culture: "Someone whispered, 'Go on and tell her, Scout.' I turned around and saw most of the town people and the entire bus delegation looking at me" (2). The community around Scout and the children her own age recognize her determination and nurturing impulse and look to her naturally to speak for them.

Today—in the twenty-first century—according to the doctrine of the country's largest Christian denomination, women cannot be leaders at church or at home. I have many dear friends who attend churches affiliated with this group, and I respect how much remarkable work is done in the name of Christ by the organization; but I find it confusing that among the denomination's core beliefs is the notion that women cannot play a role in pastoral leadership. This doctrine is ironic, first, because the divine qualities of women equip them magnificently for leadership, and because the early church actually pioneered social, racial, and gender equality unlike any movement in history. Letters from the Roman governor of Bithynia written to the emperor Trajan around AD 111 are early evidence of the revolutionary Christian movement. The governor expresses his confusion about a group of early Christians he has arrested and how to handle them, and he tells his emperor, "This made me decide it was all the more necessary to extract the truth by torture from two slave women whom they called Deaconesses."[2]

Two of the leaders in this particular church were women. I found this letter extremely fascinating. The early church saw no issue with women holding positions of power—and "slave women," at that! I am saddened to see women pastors, phenomenal speakers and leaders, who dedicate themselves to a denomination only to be relegated to less significant roles. I often wonder what the history of the church would look like if women had played a more prominent role in leadership. How many wars fought in the name of our peaceful faith could have been averted by the nurturing strength, the divine vision, and the holy compassion of women? What about the women who were leaders in the spread of the New Testament church—women like Lydia, who heard the gospel and became a key component of the church, or Junias, who Paul called, "outstanding among the apostles" (Rom. 16:7, NIV)? How can we pretend as people of faith that it is biblical to hand authority only to men as "head of the household"? How can we exclude the voices of women from our pulpits? As Eugene Peterson comments in his introduction to Galatians, "When men and women get their hands on religion, one of the first things they often do is turn it into an instrument for controlling others, either putting them or keeping them 'in their place.'"[3]

Front Porch Evenings and the Skill of Being a Girl: Women of Faith Protecting Each Other

Fortunately for Scout, she has female role models who protect her spirit from being tempered by the expectations of others. It is a necessity, articulated poignantly by Madeline Albright, who is supposed to have said that there is a special place in hell for women who do not help other women. Miss Maudie, Scout's widowed next door neighbor whose strength parallels the main protagonist, Atticus Finch, begins to take Scout under her wing early in the novel. Scout bemoans being left out of Jem and Dill's newfound companionship: "They spent days together in the tree-house plotting and planning, calling me only when they needed a third party. But I . . . spent most of the remaining twilights that summer sitting with Miss Maudie Atkinson on her front porch" (5). Maudie reaches out initially by recognizing Scout's difference and encouraging it. As their relationship begins, while other women characters call Scout by her formal name, Jean Louise, Maudie is careful to refer to her as Scout. We notice this when Maudie calls the children over for cake, "Jem Finch, Scout Finch, Charles Baker Harris, come here!" It is not until later in the novel when she has established a strong bond with Scout that she refers to her as Jean Louise. This early confirmation of Scout's uniqueness is important; I believe it is Maudie's way of affirming her. As people of faith we should also be working to recognize and encourage the strength, spirit, and God-given qualities of all people, no matter their gender.

Scout also begins to recognize the influence of her house-keeper and surrogate mother, Calpurnia, as she spends more time with her around the house, and "by watching her I began to think that there was some skill involved in being a girl" (12). Maudie and Calpurnia refuse to be defined by the gender expectations of others, protect their divine gifts, and provide a sense of shelter for Scout in the face of attacks from others. At the gathering of women for the Missionary Society meeting, we see the importance of Maudie and Calpurnia's steady influence on Scout. At the beginning of this scene, Scout has ventured into the room full of ladies in a dress and is casually asked by Miss

Maudie where her britches are. "'Under my dress.' I hadn't meant to be funny, but the ladies laughed." Scout realizes her mistake and is immediately embarrassed, but tells us, "Miss Maudie looked gravely down at me. She never laughed at me unless I meant to be funny" (24). Later in the scene, she finds comfort in Maudie's strength. Maudie grabs hold of Scout's hand and holds it securely, a gesture that provides Scout assurance in an uncomfortable situation. Scout is fostered by these women that she has grown to respect. Her strength and independence is affirmed by *their* strength.

So many great Christian books have been penned about defending the warrior spirit of men, but it is also important for women to seek out the support of other women and to pursue God's definition and vision for their lives. From the women at the Missionary Tea to the poor Mayella Ewell who seems unable to do anything on her own, it is easy for the reader to feel sorry for these women who have succumbed to the pressure of society's definitions for them. Jesus called for this type of equality in his preaching on many occasions. In Luke 13:16, after he heals a woman on the Sabbath, he refers to her as "Daughter of Abraham." "Sons of Abraham" was a common phrase at the time made in reference to male Hebrew men. Jesus is apparently the first to utter this phrase in a society where women were basically seen as slaves. With his use of the phrase *Daughter of Abraham*, he is declaring equity in a new kingdom of God. Scout respects Maudie and Calpurnia as strong independent women—women set on protecting Scout's courageous spirit.

Rescuing Tom From the Mob and Braving
the Missionary Tea: Finding Strength in Being a Lady

Scout's natural qualities inadvertently rescue the life of Tom Robinson, and possibly her father, at the jailhouse. Before the trial, Atticus, goes to the local jailhouse where Tom is being kept to make sure he is not taken by a lynch mob. In one of the great scenes of the novel, Atticus stations himself at the jailhouse door. Scout, following Jem, bursts onto the scene as Atticus stands with nothing but a newspaper against a large, angry, and drunk crowd intent on making sure that Tom never makes it to trial. First, she shows her fierce loyalty when one of the angry men grabs her brother roughly by the collar: "I kicked the man swiftly. Barefooted, I was surprised to see him fall back in real pain. I intended to kick his shin, but aimed too high." And then moments later, it is her lack of fear and vibrancy for connection with people that probably saves Tom's life. Scout examines the crowd, looking to find a familiar face. Finally she recognizes Mr. Cunningham standing in the middle of the men. Scout says hello to him but initially he pretends not to hear her. Scout continues the one-sided conversation with Mr. Cunningham about his son, Walter, and his entailment until finally, "He squatted down and took me by both shoulders. 'I'll tell him you said hey, little lady,' he said. Then he straightened up and waved a big paw. 'Let's clear out,' he called.'" (15). Slowly, as the men had arrived, they walk back to their cars and drive away from the jailhouse, leaving the Finch family and Tom Robinson safely looking on. Notice the openness Scout shows in this scene and the sincerity with which she engages Mr. Cunningham. She sees the mob not as a mindless single entity, but for who they are—individuals with families and problems of their own—and she forces them to remember their humanity.

The Missionary Society tea hosted at the Finch house ultimately acts as a milestone of Scout's journey into the world of women, and demonstrates the call for women of strength to engage their communities. Atticus arrives home and gathers with Calpurnia, Aunt Alexandra, Scout, and Maudie in the kitchen to share news of Tom Robinson's attempted escape and death at the hands of the prison guards. This intimate moment takes place in the kitchen, far from the gossiping ladies in the living room. The levity in the parlor and the emotion of the kitchen scene are meant to demonstrate the stark contrast. After Atticus leaves with Calpurnia to deliver the horrible news to Tom Robinson's wife, Alexandra sits down and puts her head in her hands. There is a long sad moment of exhaustion and silence shared by the Finch women in the quiet of the kitchen, with the ladies of the missionary tea chattering just outside the door. Alexandra begins to break down, but it is Maudie's determination that brings the women back together, and after a stirring speech about the moral strength of Atticus . . . "'Stop that shaking,' commanded Miss Maudie, and I stopped. 'Get up, Alexandra, we've left 'em long enough.' They both respond to Maudie's strength. Scout tells us that Aunt Alexandra wipes away her tears, straightens her dress, fixes her hair, and says, "'Do I show it?' 'Not a sign,' said Miss Maudie. 'Are you together again, Jean Louise?' 'Yes ma'am.' 'Then let's join the ladies,' she said grimly" (24). And so the women grace-fully work their way back into the teeth of church and society. The message in Maudie's speech to Alexandra is the message to all women who have held fast to their divine strengths. The women don't leave; they don't hide in the kitchen or cancel the meeting. They go back in and face it head on. Scout has recog-nized her own resolve in these moments and begins to appreciate the strength she sees in the women close to her. These women that she admires, although very different on the surface—Maudie, Calpurnia, even her Aunt Alexandra—display a common trait of wholly feminine power at the core of their being. It is that strength that truly signifies what it means to be a lady. As the scene closes, and the women return to the Missionary Society, serving drinks, cookies, and conversation, Scout remarks, "After all, if Aunty could be a lady at a time like this, so could I" (24).

Scout Finch, Rachel Litton, and the Feminine Expressions of Divinity

I cannot write about the strength of the women of *To Kill a Mockingbird*, or ponder the trials of Scout as she wanders through childhood sifting through the confusing expectations she calls the "pain of being called a girl" without each word delicately appended to the realities of my sister's life and her own courage. It was my own Scout Finch's bravery in the face of the terrible illness of *cardiomyopathy* that still inspires and shapes the words that I write and the life that I lead. It was my sister's vitality to press on through life until her death, continually encouraging those around her, and ardently discounting the offerings of silver-lined discouragement with an eternal resilience and optimism that changed my life. She astonished all of us in the way she systematically engaged the community around her and loved even those who had slighted her. Scout's qualities, so essential, so necessary, and so beautiful, also reflected the very nature of God in my sister's life.

I could not adequately express gratitude to the strong women in my own life—my wife, my mother, my grandmothers—who have played an essential role in shaping the way I see the world and the role of women in it. But I could never write of Scout without thoughts of my sister, Rachel, who left an indelible mark on every life she touched. She reminded all who knew her of the unique divinity and eternal strength of the feminine spirit that should be unfettered by the gender expectations of culture. This parable is written as a testament to her courage, and dedicated in her name to all of our daughters. My prayer is that they will not have their roles in life defined for them by church and society, that our "vision of their deportment" would not be limited to dresses, dolls, and their being rays of sunshine. It is my hope they would realize freedom from the confines of our starched pink cotton penitentiaries to pursue any position God calls them to, whether it is CEO, a stay-at-home mother, or even senior pastor of a church.

The Parable of Miss Maudie's Azaleas: Our Responsibility to Care for Creation

The poetry of the earth is never dead.

—JOHN KEATS (1795–1821), *ON THE GRASSHOPPER AND CRICKET*

The earth will not continue to offer its harvest, except with faithful stewardship. We cannot say we love the land and then take steps to destroy it for use by future generations.

—POPE JOHN PAUL II (1920–2005), AT A MASS FOR RURAL WORKERS, MONTEREY, CALIFORNIA, 17 SEPTEMBER 1987 audie Atkinson, one of the heroines of *To Kill a Mockingbird*, makes quite an impression on our young narrator, Scout, with her love of nature and special passion for azaleas. "Miss Maudie hated her house. Time spent indoors was time wasted . . . [She was] a chameleon lady who worked in her flowerbeds in an old straw hat and men's coveralls" (5). A good portion of the novel occurs as the children explore their world outdoors, and Maudie is the character who seems omnipresent; she watches over the street. She is simply part of the landscape, working in her yard or sitting on her porch. In fact, as Scout describes her elderly neighbor, she can't seem to do it without including something about her flowerbeds or gardening utensils.

I have always been able to identify with Maudie's love for the outdoors, and for her sentiment that time indoors is time wasted. I have a photograph from my childhood that captures this feeling. If the scene resided on a canvas beyond the confines of my own soul and required a name, I think it could be titled from the Psalmist's words, "The earth is the LORD's and everything in it" (24:1, NIV). It is an old Polaroid, a little grainy now, of my siblings and I sitting at the edge of a blacktop driveway that ran to green grass, a split-rail fence, and a sizable garden not but feet beyond. We are gathered around a chair, in which sits my father, shucking corn that he has just picked from our garden. The photo has the crisp feel of autumn, a profound lavishness in the shades of the landscape: deep greens to rich yellows to lush oranges of the sky near the well-worn white edge of its frame. My father is dressed for the cool wearing a flannel jacket, there is a mess of corn stalks lying at our feet; we are busy, we are smiling, we are outside and everything is so very obviously good.

The picture reminds me of the days when I lived life much like Jem and Scout Finch—exploring the world (within shouting distance of my house) from morning until dusk. Scout notes that she and her brother were give free rein to play anywhere in Maudie's yard, as long as they kept away from her precious azaleas. The children of *To Kill a Mockingbird* act out plays, build forts, sneak around the Radley house, and generally spend all of their free time roaming the neighborhood. There seems so much to learn outdoors. My siblings and I went digging through the field behind our yard, catching toads, snakes, bugs, learning about the plants in our family garden, exploring the scenery that surrounded our street on both sides and it was all unmistakably good.

As an educator, I find distressing how little time children have to simply investigate the natural world at their own pace. Many of them never see the outdoors, and those who do are being driven from one organized sporting competition to the next. We all need time in nature; it awakens something deep within us when we are able to connect with the natural world, to experience the majesty of a world not created by humans. To be in the presence of God's handiwork is delightfully good. The Hebrew creation story fluently explains our connection with the earth. In Genesis 2:7, the poet tells us that God sculpted man from the earth, "GOD formed Man out of dirt from the ground and blew into his nostrils the breath of life" (MSG). The parallels of the language in this text dramatically emphasize a close relationship. The Hebrew noun for man in this narrative is *adam* (a-dahm) and the word for earth, a feminine noun, is *adamah* (a-dahm-ah). In the ancient Hebrew world, a person's name was not simply an identifier, but was evocative of one's makeup. As Adam was formed from the ground, his name identifies his origins. The beautiful Old Testament understanding is that we are formed from the very substance of the earth and infused with the breath of God. We are connected to nature in an unexplainable way, and it is amazingly good. In fact, as I reflect on many of the meaningful moments of my life, I think my fondest memories took place in the outdoors. Even as a child, with all the consumer-driven anticipation of Christmas and birthday presents, I predominantly remember the simple experiences like taking walks, going sledding, pitching in on family workdays, and swimming, and all of these moments were marvelously good. I crave the outdoors as an adult. My perfect days are full of sunshine, fresh air, and my family in the beauty of nature. If I had my way, I would always rather be doing something outside.

I smiled recently to read Wendell Berry: "One of the strongest contemporary conventions is that of comparing to Thoreau every writer who has been as far out of the house as the mailbox."[1] Certainly it would seem, while I am writing, that there are days when other than my morning jog, I am barely able to make it to my own mailbox and back. I can assure you, I peek longingly through the window from my writing desk and feel much like Boo Radley, temporarily interred in my house while our children laugh and play in the beautiful Ohio summer without me. I am not sure how anyone can write of God and not reference the magnificence of creation. But I am fascinated by the nature-loving Miss Maudie and the characters found in the agricultural community of Maycomb, and I suspect that we have something to learn from their behaviors and attitudes, something that might point us toward a love and respect for nature, for God's creation. It is sublimely good to be outdoors.

Watching the Sun Go Down: Nature Is a Reflection of God's Glory

As Maudie evening observance's of nature are described by Scout, "she would appear on the porch and reign over the street in magisterial beauty" (5). Scout and Maudie develop a trust sitting together in silence observing the beauty of God's creation. Scout relates that during the summer twilights, she and Maudie would sit quietly on her porch, "watching the sky go from yellow to pink as the sun went down, watching flights of martins sweep low over the neighborhood" (5). There is truth in Scout's words. There is nothing more peaceful and magnificent than sitting on my patio and watching the colors of the Ohio summer sky slowly fade from orange to pink, from light blues to purples, a crescendo of twinkling stars and early evening moonlight accompanied softly by the orchestra of crickets. There is so much about nature that makes me awestruck and speechless; it is a spiritual quality that Ralph Waldo Emerson describes so eloquently, "Nature is too thin a screen; the glory of the omnipresent God bursts through everywhere."[2]

I vividly recall the first time I believe I genuinely felt the presence of God in nature; I was in the Andes mountains in Peru, surrounded by scenery so breathtaking that words could never do it justice. Our bus had stopped on a steep mountain pass that rested on barren and desertlike territory. I ran straight up the mountain, at least one hundred yards north of the bus, just to sit in silence and take it all in. The beauty of it was that we were traveling on a dividing line of sorts: at the bottom of our barren mountain began the jungle and the very next range of mountains were lush green and teaming with life as far as the eye could see. It was what I imagine it might look like to stand at the edges of the Garden of Eden. I don't recall now how many moments passed on that mountainside, but I will never forget the experience.

It is amazing what nature reveals about God's power and presence. "Come forth into the light of things, Let nature be your teacher,"[3] the Romantic poet William Wordsworth says, evoking the thoughts of David the psalmist, who tells us that "the heavens declare the glory of God; the skies proclaim the work of his hands. Day after day they pour forth speech; night after night they display knowledge. There is no speech or language where their voice is not heard. Their voice goes out into all the earth, their words to the ends of the world" (Ps. 19:1–4, NIV). This "voice" I imagine to be the breath caught when peering at the Grand Canyon; it is the sense of smallness felt driving through the Smokey Mountains; it is the feeling of vibrancy as sunshine sparkles through the grass and breath comes in puffs of smoke on that first morning of frost. Nature with all of its beauty reminds us that we are small, that we are subject to the same biological, chemical, and environmental forces as all other living creatures. Even more important, though, it shouts that we must drop the pretense of our own godliness. It humbles us with simple sunsets or magnificent thunderstorms, and is our constant indication of the interconnectedness of all things; it is a reflection of the Triune God who lives in relationship.

I often wonder if we can maintain a healthy soul without finding quiet time outdoors. I love that it is a tree the secretive Boo Radley uses to communicate with the Finch children. Scout and Jem notice the gifts left for them by Boo Radley in the knothole of an oak tree they must pass by every day on their way to and from school. For me, creation is a direct reflection of God, and it is hard to imagine experiencing God without the beauty all around me. From a jog one Indian summer afternoon to a bike ride on a remote trail, nature is often the vocabulary God uses to speak to me. But I believe that scripture points to the power of creation as a reflection of God too: "For since the creation of the world God's invisible qualities—his eternal power and divine nature—have been clearly seen, being understood from what has been made, so that men are without excuse" (Romans 1:20, NIV). To experience nature is to witness the fullness of the presence of God; nature teaches us the glory of the Creator so that we may believe, and observing nature is a form of true worship.

The Flowers Are Going to Hell Too:
Our Attitudes Toward Nature

In a conversation about religion, Maudie tells Scout about some of the Maycomb church folks who pass by her house. They seem to take issue with her lifestyle, she explains, saying that they "told me me and my flowers were going to hell?' 'Your flowers, too?' 'Yes ma'am. They'd burn right with me. They thought I spent too much time in God's outdoors and not enough time inside the house reading the Bible'" (5). I love how Maudie connects "God's outdoors" with being indoors reading the Bible—almost as if she places equal value on both exercises. Maybe our outlook on faith affects our attitude toward the earth.

Songwriter Linford Detweiler of Over the Rhine recently posted a letter on his Web site, ruminating about his farm in Ohio: "I remember wondering aloud after we had our first garden out here about whether the church had missed a sin. The pleasure of cupping ones hand around the smooth underbelly of a vine-ripened tomato is about as blood red sensual as it gets. Yep, they might have forgotten to forbid that one."[4] It reminds me of Miss Maudie's attitude toward the church people passing by her yard. There is something sensual about nature, and it makes me wonder if we really haven't forgotten that our purpose is to enjoy the goodness of creation. The lines from Psalm 104 remind us of the splendor of nature and that the Creator's fingerprint is all over it: "He waters the mountains from his upper chambers; the earth is satisfied by the fruit of his work. He makes grass grow for the cattle, and plants for man to cultivate—bringing forth food from the earth: wine that gladdens the heart of man, oil to make his face shine, and bread that sustains his heart" (vv. 13–15, NIV).

Yet I grew up an evangelical subculture and have listened to many good folks talk of "this world" with so much lamentation in their voice. Like Andy Dufresne from Stephen King's *Rita Hayworth and the Shawshank Redemption*, they are just biding their time until escape. Some are closed off from placing value on their relationships and the beauty of nature around them. They believe they have punched their ticket to the sweet by and by and aren't concerned about tossing their trash out of the window on the train ride home. They have little concern about the world they will leave for their children or the quality of existence they are creating for their neighbors. Our attitudes and understandings about the symbiotic characteristics of the natural world are slowly progressing, but I am afraid that some people of faith (like the ones passing by Miss Maudie's yard) have missed the mark with their attitudes toward nature. I have certainly come a long way to understanding my personal accountability in these matters of creation.

I remember hiking along a river in Illinois at a beautiful state park with a friend. It was a stunning fall day, the air was crisp, the leaves were gold, and the sound of the water rushing over the rocks floated up into the trees and echoed all around us. In my youthful ignorance, I made the mistake of discarding an empty bag of chips *somewhere* along the hiking trail. This act of littering went temporarily unnoticed by my hiking partner, but when she realized what I had done, she was furious. I remember her complete irritation with me, the lecture that ensued, and her refusal to leave the park until I had retread and retraced our steps, scouring God's freaking-green hiking trail for over forty-five minutes until I could finally produce my trash and rescue some poor raccoon from an addiction to junk food. It's a funny memory, but in reality, my friend was right. Leaving human trash on the trail was destructive, my attitude was selfish, and, furthermore, I was being a dreadful neighbor. I wasn't setting out to hurt the environment, but I certainly wasn't conscious of my responsibility to care for it. Our dismissive attitude toward nature has a profound effect; we were called to be good stewards of this earthly garden.

Today we are faced with the reality that we have not cared for the environment properly. We *are* responsible for alterations in the atmosphere. Nitrogen oxides and sulfur dioxide emissions have increased steadily; as a result asthma cases are dramatically on the rise in otherwise perfectly healthy children around the world. Our waterways are horribly polluted and it is estimated that close to one billion people in the world do not have access to clean water. In my own home state of Ohio, there are over one hundred endangered species. Two large islands of plastic waste float in the Pacific Ocean slowly decaying into a toxic soup. Both are the size of the state of Texas and growing—we currently call them the Western and Eastern Pacific Garbage Patches. The relentless consumption of energy in first-world countries has produced severe repercussions on the quality of life of our neighbors in third world countries: pollution, starvation, slavery, nothing short of a silent brutality. The conservationist Wendell Berry reminds us, "I believe that until fairly recently our destructions of nature were more or less unwitting - - the by-products, so to speak, of our ignorance or weakness or depravity. It is our present principled and elaborately rationalized rape and plunder of the natural world that is a new thing under the sun."[5] Have we forgotten the "goodness" of Genesis 1? Will God hold us accountable for not proving trustworthy to manage this beautiful world? Like my reminiscence of our family garden, God's glory is reflected in all of creation and it is good. Miss Maudie's statement to Scout is ripe with the sorrow that we have forgotten the importance of God's earth, and it is filled with the affirmation that "all things were created by him [Christ] and for him" (Col. 1:16, NIV). The biblical narrative makes it clear that we have a responsibility to the earth, to restore creation. Taking care of the environment has become so politicized that we have forgotten that caring for creation is truly synonymous with caring for our neighbors. Nature is not just a reflection of the Creator; it is the very manifestation of His glory.

Keeping the Flowers Warm, Our Responsibility to Care for Creation

During an unusual cold snap in Maycomb, the children watch intently as Miss Maudie works in her yard to carefully wrap several small bushes in burlap bags. Jem inquires why. "'Keep 'em warm,' she said." Not satisfied with Maudie's answer Jem presses on—he wants to understand the science behind what Maudie is doing. She responds, "I cannot answer that question, Jem Finch. All I know is if it freezes tonight these plants'll freeze, so you cover 'em up"(8).

Maudie feels a responsibility to care for her plants. The why of things is a mystery to her; she just knows it is her duty to do it, and she carries out her task with a nurturing spirit. We no longer can claim ignorance of this duty. "We have lived by the assumption that what was good for us would be good for the world . . . We have been wrong. We must change our lives, so that it will be possible to live by the contrary assumption that what is good for the world will be good for us. And that requires that we make the effort to know the world and learn what is good for us."[6] Why we should cover the plants from the cold is no longer a mystery to us; we are now armed with the scientific justifications to care for creation. I can't get away from the thought that it might be our obligation as people of God to use fewer chemicals, to drive less, to plant and nurture trees, to cut back on our energy consumption, to learn to work the land, to get dirt under our fingernails, and to let creation teach us a thing or two.

Could there be spiritual power in simply keeping a garden? A friend of mine pastors in Oxford, Mississippi, where he began a community garden at his church several years ago, encouraging his congregation to get out and engage their little plot of land. Many of those who joined him in the processes of the garden have also been led to move toward a life of conservation. Working outside together has bolstered their community and has benefited the neighborhood of his church. Gardening leads to concern for the earth; it seems that once we make an investment in the soil, we cannot help but be caught up in the miracles of creation. I listened last spring as my friend preached a beautiful sermon series titled "Lessons from the Garden," marveling at how our society has changed from agricultural to consumer driven, from community oriented to transient, and from patient understanding of the rhythms of life to the frenetic impatience of a fast-food world.

Maudie is out working in her yard to protect her plants and flowers from an unusual South Alabama cold snap. Anyone who has dirtied his fingers with sweet soil in an attempt to make something grow will realize his relationship to the earth. In fact, the Bible points clearly to our bond to the earth in both renditions of creation. In Genesis 1: "God spoke: 'Let us make human beings in our image, make them reflecting our nature So they can be responsible for the fish in the sea, the birds in the air, the cattle . . . and every animal that moves on the face of the Earth" (v. 26, MSG). And yes, caretakers of the earth itself. Genesis 2:15 (MSG) continues: "God took the Man and set him down in the Garden of Eden to work the ground and keep it in order." The commands are as clear as Miss Maudie's determination to save her azaleas from the cold. We are accountable for creation. I suspect it is theologically irresponsible to treat the earth as a place we will leave one day, never to return, without thought of our brothers and sisters who will inhabit it afterward, without realizing that nature is the very reflection of God, that the first command to humanity was to care for creation, without deploring the environmental oppression our consumerism has leveled on our less affluent neighbors. It should be our vocation to cover our plants from the cold.

Red Geraniums and Untended Land,
Caring for Creation Builds Hope and Community

While Miss Maudie is our model of a responsible attitude toward nature, it is several of the Maycomb residents that reflect how that investment in the earth can be beneficial. Early in the book Scout discusses a neighboring farmer's struggle to keep his land during the Great Depression. She tells us that Maycomb County was predominantly farm country, and money was scarce for everyone; she goes on to say, "Mr. Cunningham could get a WPA job, but his land would go to ruin if he left it, and he was willing to go hungry to keep his land" (2). Mr. Cunningham *will not leave* his land. I wonder how much our transiency—a reflection of our values—has influenced our attitudes toward creation. It is implied in these lines that if Mr. Cunningham leaves his land for a WPA job to support his family, his land would go to waste. His connection to the land would be severed; he would lose his identity, it would alter his very being.

His investment in the land is also an investment in community. My friend Jason is a mad-scientist organic farmer and environmental sage who dabbles in everything from raising chickens to cooking bio-diesel fuel, but one of the most remarkable things about his ministry is what it has done for the community around him. Jason has moved his family into an economically challenged neighborhood and has begun planting a community garden on his street. He teaches children in the inner city how to care for these gardens. We have watched with amazement as his neighborhood's investment in the soil of their community is leading to a revitalized street. When we make an investment in the land, we are also investing in our neighbors. Jason is restoring creation in his neighborhood—which is returning a sense of community. Beautiful things are happening there.

Scout tells us that there was something about the unkempt Ewell house that puzzled the residents of Maycomb. "Against the fence, in a line, were six chipped-enamel slop jars holding brilliant red geraniums, cared for as tenderly as if they belonged to Miss Maudie Atkinson . . . People said they were Mayella Ewell's" (17). Mayella is the lonely and pathetic character who falsely accuses the innocent Tom Robinson of raping her. She is sexually abused by her own father. She is a complete social outcast with no friends. Her life is miserable. She lives in a house full of children right next to a trash dump. Curiously, the only thing appealing about the Ewell home is a row of red geraniums that Mayella tends. Taking care of creation is more than just our responsibility, it is essential to our emotional well-being. Although it is never really discussed in the novel, I have always had the sense that the geraniums are the only beautiful and hopeful things in Mayella's life.

I believe that there is something inherent to our very humanity that finds hope in nurturing the fragile beauty of nature. For years mental health professionals have discussed a connection between gardening and improvement in a number of different disorders. Gardening is a proven stress-relieving activity—many hospitals are planting gardens now because studies have shown them to both relieve tension and encourage social interaction. Many of us, like Mayella, can probably find some peace from our hectic lives by spending some time in the garden. There is a sense of hope found in planting seeds, and nurturing them to health and beauty. I wonder if this isn't how Mayella survives through her terrible home life.

Loving a Bigger Yard: Caring for Nature is Spiritual

"She [Miss Maudie] loved everything that grew in God's earth, even the weeds" (5). Maudie's focus on nature has always interested me because she is clearly one of the protagonists of the book. Her intention to care for the creation around her is simply a way of life for her. So it should be for us: not something that dominates our lives, but an ethic that is lived out as a response to God's grace. The role that Maudie exhibits for us is that of caretaker to the earth. It is her love for it and her passion to toil in it that exhibits an understanding of the close connection we have to the natural world. Not only does the creation story in Genesis clearly articulate our responsibility to the environment, but it also shows us that creation is good. The word *good* is repeated more times in the first two chapters of Genesis to describe creation than it is used in the entire rest of the Bible's first book. Miss Maudie's character exhibits our role as gardeners, as good stewards, as the caretakers of creation.

When her house burns down, the children come over to help her clean up in the aftermath of the fire. Maudie affirms her love for nature in her response to Jem and Scout about the tragedy: "Always wanted a smaller house . . . Gives me more yard . . . I'll have more room for my azaleas now!" (8). Rather than lamenting her loss of the material, she is celebrating the opportunity to have more nature surrounding her. With a hopeful smile, Maudie tells the children of her plans to build a smaller house, where she'll still have the nicest yard in the entire state of Alabama.

While not all of us practice the care of creation, we are all somehow cognizant of our deep connection to it. Not long ago I took a group of students outside for a creative writing assignment. As they read their completed projects to the class, I was taken back at the theme of spirituality that permeated every single reading. My mother recounts sitting in my dad's office every day through the months after his death. She remembers watching the stillness of the winter world through that window each afternoon, wondering how she would go on. She remembers watching as the cold slowly gave way to spring, the flowers began to bloom, and nature set in motion to sprout forth into the colors of life. Somehow, in the observance of nature's rhythms of resilience and rebirth, she discovered the hope to continue on.

I believe that God will hold us accountable for what we have been given to nurture and care for—His garden. It is our responsibility to worship God by helping care for and restore the good to our planet—not just for ourselves, but for our neighbors and the future generations who will pass through this grand playground, that they may find the both the truths and the glory of the omnipresent God still veiled in its beauty and power. Mrs. Maudie and the people of Maycomb point us toward a love for creation and an obligation to prove ourselves trustworthy with God's gift. Creation is the hope of red geraniums, the beauty of azaleas (and even weeds); it is the spiritualism of being present in nature, and it is the majesty of sunsets and mountains; it is our constant reminder of new life. It is our obligation to respond as good stewards of this holy gift.

The Parable of Atticus Finch:
The Model of Christian Courage

*It is curious—curious that physical courage should be
so common in the world, and moral courage so rare.*

—MARK TWAIN (1835–1910), AMERICAN AUTHOR AND HUMORIST

*One isn't necessarily born with courage, but one is born
with potential. Without courage, we cannot practice
any other virtue with consistency. We can't be kind,
true, merciful, generous, or honest.*

—MAYA ANGELOU (B. 1928), AMERICAN POET AND MEMOIRIST

I t is a moment for the big screens of Hollywood: one man standing up against an angry crowd to save the life of another. "'You know what we want,' another man said. 'Get aside from the door, Mr. Finch.' . . . 'You can turn around and go home again, Walter, Atticus said pleasantly" (15). The scene might be the pinnacle of heroism for Atticus Finch, the novel's protagonist. It is these moments of courage that are captured and glorified by our culture, but the greater lesson is always found when we examine the entire story. Pick up the paper, turn on a television set, or open up a history book—the world is moved forward by courage. Scripture is full of verses that call us toward this ethic: "Be strong and courageous . . . do not be discouraged, for the LORD your God will be with you wherever you go" (Joshua 1:9, NIV).

There is something divine when a human being stretches out toward courage. In *To Kill a Mockingbird*, courage is personified by Atticus Finch, a lawyer, father, and representative in the Alabama state legislature who has a sincere aversion to practicing criminal law. He has taken on the responsibility of defending an African-American man falsely accused of rape in a culture, a time, and town where racism is so prevalent that he calls it Maycomb's "usual disease." His willingness to defend the innocent Tom Robinson unleashes a torrent of animosity toward his family that even extends to his young children, Scout and Jem. Atticus's stunning representation of courage is so simple and so utterly profound, that it hardly needs further discussion. Yet he views his actions not as heroism, but as his personal responsibility. Miss Maudie explains the situation to Jem and Scout, "I simply want to tell you that there are some men in this world who were born to do our unpleasant jobs for us. Your father's one of them" (22).

This literary character leaps from the pages of the novel and has an enormous impact in our modern world. He is frequently discussed in law schools across the country as a hero of litigation; in fact, in 1997 the Alabama State Bar created a monument in his honor and dubbed him "the first commemorative milestone in the state's judiciary history."[1] Some have called him the Abe Lincoln of Alabama. He has been voted by the American Film Institute (over characters like Superman or Batman) as the greatest American hero of twentieth-century film. And yet I have a strong suspicion that this would all be an embarrassing nuisance to him. The narrator, Scout, explains the mundane work of this hero early in the novel. His sparsely decorated office is certainly nothing impressive. He mainly enjoys helping the townfolk sort out their economic problems, and certainly doesn't have an impressive record when it comes to criminal law, as Scout points out: "His first two clients were the last two persons hanged in the Maycomb County jail"(1). Atticus does not aspire to heroism; he is simply a man who chooses to do what is right.

The Bravest Man Who ever Lived: Courage Is the Decision to Put Others First

It is not Atticus the superhero, but an ordinary guy who is a model of courage. The word *courage* gets thrown around quite liberally by our culture. One of my favorite football players was tragically murdered the other summer. As a member of the community, he was responsible for so much philanthropy, but I cringed a bit to hear *courage* bantered about to describe his performance . . . on the football field? Think of all the trivial exploits we label courageous. Our culture defines courage as power, as winning, as complete fearlessness, and we celebrate it when it is noticed. But when true courage happens, there are rarely trumpets sounding, news cameras rolling, or awards banquets planned to rejoice it.

When I consider courage, I think about the exceptional men and women who place themselves in uniforms and sacrifice their lives for their country—for others. I contemplate the sacrifice of women like Rosa Parks, the consternation of men like Abraham Lincoln, or the determination of Martin Luther. I think of our friend Jen, who lives out a beautiful joy that is contagious to all who know her in the face of one really scary word—cancer. I also think about my mom learning to live without my dad, who died at a very young age, and then having to cope with the loss of her daughter, or my brother-in-law and his struggle to move on after his world was turned upside down by death of my sister and their baby. I think of leaders in the early church, common men and women—stoned to death, crucified, and tortured for their belief in the One who is the truest measure of courage.

But I am often reminded of a small town lawyer, an average guy, a good neighbor in Maycomb, Alabama, who had never won a criminal case. When I contemplate what courage should look like to us, I think of Atticus Finch—not Atticus the hero, but the fifty-year-old man whose daily grace, wisdom, patience, and faith has so much to teach us. It is an ethic he displays in his day-to-day interactions with his belligerent neighbor, Mrs. Dubose, the elderly woman who torments his children. Scout is terrified of the woman, and is awestruck at her father's kindness as he interacts with her: "It was times like these when I thought my father, who hated guns and had never been to any wars, was the bravest man who had ever lived" (11). Atticus Finch teaches us that courage is far more than one heroic moment; it is a way of life and a principal guided by our faith in someone greater than ourselves. So it is about the narrative of Atticus's life that we ask the questions: What does courage really mean? What does it look like? How does it happen?

Mad Dogs and Morphine Habits:
True Courage Doesn't Begin With Power

When we look to Scripture for models of courage, it is astounding to discover that the men and women we believe embody this quality actually led very dubious lives. Abraham was unquestionably afraid and lied about his wife; Moses was certainly not courageous when he murdered a soldier and fled Egypt, or when he pleaded with God to find someone more qualified to speak with the Pharaoh. Jonah undoubtedly ran away from God's message and had quite a few strange experiences in the process; Esther had no intention of marrying a king and feared for her own well-being; and Elijah, a man who witnessed God bring down fire from the sky, was quick to run and hide in a cave when the chips were down. It is interesting to consider how ordinary, unexceptional, incapable, and human they seem in their respective journeys. These biblical characters do not reflect the power and heroism that we often associate with courage; in fact, a closer examination of their life stories reveals that they are rather common folks—like you and me.

At the beginning of the tenth chapter, Scout explains that from her and Jem's perspective, there is not much to brag about when it comes to their father. "Atticus was feeble, he was nearly fifty . . . He was much older than the parents of our school contemporaries, and there was nothing Jem or I could say about him when our classmates said, '*My* father—'" (10). It is one February day when Jem and Scout are playing outside that they notice a dog, Old Tim Johnson, wandering down the street. The dog is rabid, and Jem delivers a hilarious explanation to Calpurnia in which he twists, gulps, hunches his shoulders, and does his best to mimic the behavior of the oncoming threat. Calpurnia first warns the neighbors, and then calls Atticus home from his office. Her panic over the situation adds to the drama of the scene. This event is a fearful one for Scout and Jem, who are elementary-age children. Sure enough, the mad dog is slowly working its way toward their home. The scene is monumental in Scout's eyes. Atticus zooms into the driveway in a black Ford, with Maycomb's sheriff, Mr. Heck Tate. They walk toward the street to observe the oncoming threat and then, to the surprise of the children, Mr. Tate pleads with Atticus to take his rifle and shoot the dog. Atticus refuses again, contending that he hasn't shot a gun in many years. Scout recounts the action in tones of enchantment. Mr. Tate hastily hands the rifle to her father and implores him to take the shot. "With movements so swift they seemed simultaneous, Atticus's hand yanked the ball-tipped lever as he brought the gun to his shoulder. The rifle cracked." (10). With one shot, Atticus kills the rabid dog. The children, who have been practicing with air rifles they received from their uncle for Christmas, are astonished by their father's aptitude with a gun. In fact, Jem is left speechless. They learn from Miss Maudie that their father was once know as the best shot in Maycomb County and the chapter closes with their believing that their father's talent can make them proud.

At this point in the novel, with the Tom Robinson trial on the horizon and the Finch family facing the fury of the town, it is reassuring to know that Atticus can handle a gun. In my first read of the novel, I remember thinking that this was a clear sign that Atticus had the ability to take care of himself; after all, heroes have the power to do that type of thing. It was a comforting thought to a young reader concerned for the safety of the Finch family. Scout had been struck with terror about the approaching mad dog, and certainly through her eyes, it took courage for Atticus to walk into the middle of the street wielding a gun and face the terror down.

Shortly after this event, the children encounter someone who appears almost as terrible as a mad dog: "neighborhood opinion was that Mrs. Dubose was the meanest old woman who had ever lived" (4). Scout explains that Jem would not go near her house without Atticus close by. The ailing and elderly Mrs. Henry

Lafayette Dubose curses at them and hassles them each day as they walk by her house. They fear her, and that dread is heightened by the neighborhood legend that she keeps an old World War I pistol hidden beneath her shawl while lording over the street corner from her front porch. Her constant goading finally breaks Jem; he tears up the flowers in her front yard. As discipline, Atticus makes the children go read to Mrs. Dubose each evening after school. It is not until after Mrs. Dubose dies that the children learn the extent of her illness; she'd been working her way through a terrible addiction to morphine prescribed for a painful ailment. Atticus uses this honest moment to help Scout and Jem understand the true qualities of courage. With the events of the mad dog fresh in their minds, and a sincere distaste for the old woman who had tormented them, Atticus explains to his children his deep respect for Mrs. Dubose. "I wanted you to see what real courage is, instead of getting the idea that courage is a man with a gun in his hand. It's when you know you're licked before you begin but you begin anyway and you see it through no matter what."(11). He goes on to say that even if the children hadn't gotten into trouble with Mrs. Dubose, he had planned on making them read to her anyway. This scene, more than any other, cuts to the essence of courage and demonstrates that it is not found in the power of a gun or in the confirmation of victory. No, courage is a decision, and it is a spiritual quality that goes far beyond our trendy and generous use of the term. Atticus shows the children that courage has little to do with power, and everything to do with making the decision to do what is right . . . win or lose.

It is this quality that led the apostles Peter and John, after they had been beaten and warned not to speak of Jesus to anyone, to defy the high priests of Jerusalem. "They called them back and warned them that they were on no account ever again to speak or teach in the name of Jesus. But Peter and John spoke right back, 'Whether it's right in God's eyes to listen to you rather than God, you decide. As for us, there's no question—we can't keep quiet about what we've seen and heard" (Acts 4:18–20, MSG). Notice one of them was Peter, a man who failed his tests of courage and denied Jesus three times. Yet Peter was called the Rock, and was considered the father of the church, the foundation of the new body of believers who followed Jesus. It is not the power, but the simple conviction and courage in the decisions of these average fishermen that help build a strong foundation for the early church.

Meeting the Lynch Mob With a Newspaper: Courage Isn't the Absence of Fear, but the Absence of Self

One of the greatest scenes in the novel takes place when Atticus leaves the house one evening with only a chair, a light bulb, and a newspaper, heading down to the city jail to sit outside and watch over Tom Robinson. The curious children sneak out of the house to follow him, where they see their father standing down a lynch mob of angry men who have come to take Tom. Scout bursts through the crowd of men and runs up to her father. "'I thought I would have a fine surprise, but his face killed my joy. A flash of plain fear was going out of his eyes . . ." (15). So this is courage. Scout breaks into the clearing to find Atticus standing between the door to the jailhouse and a large group of men intent on ending Tom Robinson's life, and the first thing she notices is the fear in her father's eyes. Atticus's fear is certainly for his own children, whose arrival has completely surprised him, but I think it would be foolish to assume that he is not fearful for his own safety and Tom Robinson's as well.

Gregory Peck won an Academy Award for his role as Atticus Finch in the renowned film version of the novel. He cherished his role as Atticus and frequently said it was the greatest part he had ever played. I generally agree; he is an amazing Atticus Finch. However, I have always had one minor objection to his portrayal that he could do nothing to change. When Peck played the role, he was a tall, athletic, and capable presence on screen. His magnificent stature is so formidable in the film that there are times I often wonder how he might be intimidated by anyone. For all of the undeniable beauty and passion of his performance, I have always felt that his height detracted a little from the courage of the character. While I can't imagine anyone else playing the role, I envisioned the Atticus who ventures out to face an angry, drunk, and potentially violent lynch mob as a slight, older gentleman, one so average that he could not physically dissuade anyone.

Adding to the intensity of this scene is the reality that Atticus, a man known as the deadest shot in Maycomb, comes to the jail to protect Tom Robinson with a newspaper and a light. This is the soul of real courage played out before our eyes: Atticus is unarmed, and is certainly not devoid of fear. Scout goes on to describe the confrontation, telling us her father rose slowly from the chair, as if he were an old man: "He put his newspaper down very carefully, adjusting his creases with lingering fingers. They were trembling a little" (15). It is a frail and older Atticus who faces the mob with a radical courage of nonviolence. He is a man who probably walked to the jail with the understanding that he could be physically harmed. His hands are shaking; his expression is full of fear. This scene makes it plain that there is more to courage than simply overcoming fear—it is willingly placing ourselves at risk in order to save another. This image of Atticus standing his ground with hands trembling reminds me of one of my favorite Bible stories, from the book of Daniel.

Three of the king's most valued servants are placed on trial by jealous advisors for not bowing down and worshipping the image of their leader. The king calls the three servants before him and demands that they bow down and worship his image instead of their own God. If they refuse, he will have them executed by way of a fiery furnace. These three friends—Shadrach, Meshach, and Abednego—are discussed in Sunday school lessons the world over because of the miraculous result of their trial. When King Nebuchadnezzar commands them to be thrown into a fire (so hot that it kills the soldiers who are escorting them), the three are saved from the inferno by an angel of God. But the true power of the story, the true measure of courage—like Atticus at the jailhouse—is revealed earlier in the tale. "'Is it true, Shadrach, Meshach, and Abednego, that you don't respect my gods and refuse to worship the gold statue that I have set up?' I'm giving you a second chance . . . If you don't worship it, you will be pitched into a roaring furnace, no questions asked'" (Dan. 3:13, MSG). Just as Atticus stands defenseless before the angry lynch mob, the three friends stand powerless before the king. I imagine that it is through shaking voices, trembling hands, and eyes full of fear that they deliver their response with one voice. "Your threat means nothing to us. If you throw us into the fire, the God we serve can rescue us from your roaring furnace and anything else you might cook up, O king" (v. 16). And then they deliver some of the most courageous lines found in the Bible, "But even if he doesn't, it wouldn't make a bit of difference, O king. We still wouldn't serve your gods or worship the gold statue you set up" (v. 16).

Courage is a decision. I once heard pastor Erwin McManus say that courage isn't the absence of fear, but the absence of self. Both Atticus and these three servants of King Nebuchadnezzar demonstrate that the essence of courage is indeed the absence of self.

Bob Ewell's Threatening Presence: Sometimes Courage Means Walking Out Your Front Door

After the Tom Robinson trial is over, Bob Ewell is relegated again to the town dump and viewed by most of the locals with utter disdain. The Ewell family is treated as almost less than human. Even though Atticus lost the trial, Bob Ewell still feels slighted at the embarrassment he believes Atticus and Judge Taylor have caused him, and he makes it clear that he is out to get Atticus. Bob Ewell stops Atticus near the post office, threatens him, and spits in his face. In the very next lines, we learn more about the incident: "'I wish Bob Ewell wouldn't chew tobacco,' was all Atticus said about it" (22). This scene demonstrates a meaning of courage that is beyond anything I have experienced. As Scout tells the story, our admiration for Atticus's courage continues to grow: "Miss Stephanie said Atticus didn't bat an eye, just took out his handkerchief and wiped his face and stood there and let Mr. Ewell call him names" (23). I wonder if our culture would call that response courage. Most of us would like to see Atticus take him out, right on the post office steps. Bystanders in this scene might even call Atticus cowardly, but he is demonstrating a deeper courage by walking away from potential violence, turning the other cheek.

Atticus continues on with the business of life, although the threats leveled by Bob Ewell toward him mirror the fears in the lives of many. I read recently that over twenty-four million Americans suffer from some type of anxiety disorder (10 percent of the population); this makes it one of the most diagnosed medical problems in our country. Thus for many reading this book, courage, in a very real sense, might be just mustering the strength to walk out the front door in the morning. I have friends who must take medication and commit to a good deal of prayer to cope with onsets of anxiety. We live in a world of terror alerts, flu pandemics, and warning labels. Our culture is changing so rapidly and buzzing with a demand for constant connection that it is unusual not to be a little unsettled. Anxiety is becoming a norm, a new reality of our postmodern existence. Although Atticus denies any concern as he discusses the situation with Jem and Scout (in an attempt to allay their fears), I am sure he has some unease. He is probably wary of Bob Ewell, but he never allows it to consume his daily life. He appears to be grounded in a trust that he never quite explains, but it is the same trust that prompts him to walk away from Bob Ewell's threats at the post office.

It is clear that the apprehension of our own Bob Ewell lurking around the corner has a dramatic impact on the way we live our lives. Remember, God calls us to live in the moment. "Therefore I tell you, do not worry about your life, what you will eat or drink; or about your body, what you will wear . . . Look at the birds of the air; they do not sow or reap or store away in barns, and yet your heavenly Father feeds them. Are you not much more valuable than they?" (Matthew 6:25–26, NIV).

We seem to live in a culture consumed with fear. I read a shocking article recently: the pastor of a congregation in Atlanta told a prominent newspaper that he was planning to hire armed security guards in an effort to protect his parishioners during worship time. I wonder if part of courage is simply taking the small steps out of our front door, putting one foot in front of the other and going about the business of life with a trust in God. Part of trusting Him is realizing how to live in the face of these fears. I am relatively sure that our sources of fear in the postmodern world are not likely to recede anytime soon.

Subsequently, the threats to Atticus continue when Bob Ewell, during his weekly visit to the welfare office, loudly blames Atticus for his perpetual state of joblessness. "Atticus told Mrs. Ruth not to fret, if Bob Ewell wanted to discuss Atticus 'getting' his job, he knew the way to the office'" (27). There is more to Atticus than just optimism. He goes about his business normally, despite the threats from Bob Ewell. Oftentimes true courage is just that simple. It is the straightforward hope found in moving forward in our lives with trust. But the threats from Bob Ewell quickly evolve into another pressing discussion of courage, as Jem and Scout discuss how their father should protect himself against this menace.

The Deadest Shot in Maycomb Without a Gun: Divine Courage Isn't Violent

Scout and Jem, enamored by their father's prowess with a gun and worried about Bob Ewell's threats, try to persuade Atticus to carry one for protection. Jem observes that their father does not own a gun, and remembers that he did not carry one to the jailhouse to protect Tom Robinson. But Scout is not satisfied. "'This is different,' I said. 'We can ask him to borrow one.' We did, and he said, 'Nonsense'" (23). Atticus rejects the temptation to guard himself with popular culture's definition of power in this scene. He scoffs at the idea of using power for protection. He will not carry a gun. Society would dictate that we respond to threats with an equal and measured strength. This is the great impasse in the novel's discussion of courage. It is where the definition of pop-culture courage meets a more eternal characterization of the noble idea—the one found in Scripture.

Courage constitutes a much different type of action than the world at large can understand. Jesus, the commander-in-chief of courage, was a King whom many of His followers believed would overthrow the oppressive Roman government and reestablish Israel as an independent state. He embodied true courage. Although He clearly prepared His followers for the moment, it was not until the experience at the Garden of Gethsemane, when soldiers sent from the church of Israel came to arrest him, that the disciples began to understand. Three of the Gospels tell us a disciple of Jesus (presumably Peter) cut the ear off of a man (a servant of the high priest) during the attempt to arrest Jesus. In all three accounts, Jesus rebuked the violent act. But the Gospel of Luke tells us that Jesus healed the ear of the servant. "When Jesus' followers saw what was going to happen, they said, 'Lord, should we strike with our swords?' And one of them struck the servant of the high priest, cutting off his right ear. But Jesus answered, 'No more of this!' And he touched the man's ear and healed him'" (Luke 22:49–51, NIV). (I feel a little like the disciples in this scene sometimes. It seems completely natural to want to respond with violence in defense of myself and my family.) In all of the Gospel narratives, there is the intimation that right at this moment, Jesus' followers scatter. I believe that despite His teaching, they misunderstood His intentions, and when He makes it clear that he is not going fight the battle with violence, it sends them temporarily into confusion, fleeing into the night.

I think it is deeper than a call to pacifism; Jesus' course of action is the most defining moment of courage in the history of the world, one that takes power from the hands of violence and places it squarely in the corner of self-sacrifice; it is a reordering of the world that only those who walk in His footsteps can understand.

Similarly, it is a very Christlike moment when Atticus rejects the power of the gun for defense, just as it baffles us that he walks away from being threatened and spit on at the post office. It is a courage that doesn't always win the day, yet when we see it happen, something deep within our soul cries out that it is true. This is the type of courage that makes us realize there is something divine hidden in the DNA of humanity. We long to see this, and when we do we celebrate it with sainthood and statues. Courage is the divine quality that we celebrate in leaders like Gandhi and Martin Luther King Jr. For each of us, though, it is as simple and practical as choosing to avoid retaliating with the power of our words, choosing to walk away from confrontation, accepting a loss for the sake of peace. Atticus's decision to shun power in response to Bob Ewell is a clear reflection of the divine nature of courage. But a quality as clear and defined as courage can also be quite complicated at times.

Protecting Children and Boo Radley:
Courage Means Defending the Powerless

Perhaps in every situation our goal should be to pursue courage with the pacifism of Jesus' response to threats and injustice, but I struggle with this concept when it comes to the powerless and the oppressed. In every way, I believe that to follow Jesus is to swear off the earthly practices of power and violence; but I also wrestle with what it means to possess that worldly power and stand idle while the innocent suffer. In the dramatic conclusion of *To Kill a Mockingbird*, Bob Ewell does not make good on his threats to Atticus. Rather, the drunken antagonist attacks Atticus's defenseless children with a knife under the cover of darkness. And it is at this point in the novel that the mysterious Boo Radley emerges from his house to save them. The struggle is violent: Ewell breaks young Jem Finch's arm and leaves him unconscious. As he turns to attack Scout, Boo comes to the rescue. While we are not given a clear account of the action, it is evident that Boo kills Bob Ewell in his struggle to save the lives of Jem and Scout. In the aftermath of the scuffle, Sheriff Heck Tate and Atticus discuss the events of the evening and how they will deal with what happened. Scout recounts the intensity of the conversation as Heck Tate makes it clear that Bob Ewell has been killed with a kitchen knife, adding, "that Atticus wasn't going to stand there and maintain that any boy Jem's size with a busted arm had fight enough left in him to tackle and kill a grown man" (30).

This sequence highlights a struggle in my faith about courage that I am not certain will ever be reconciled. Boo's courage spurs him into action, and it is violent. I grapple with the idea that it is by violence that these children, incapable of defending themselves, are saved from the evil of Bob Ewell. We have considered the truths of courage as nonviolent, walking away from conflict.

Does this, then, detract from the courage of Boo Radley? Try to imagine Boo Radley observing *his* children in peril from behind the edges of closed shutters. Is his intent to kill Bob Ewell? I believe that the courage is not found in the violence of the scene, but in Boo's intent to rescue the powerless children. When I consider the dichotomies of courage and violence in this light, it often reminds me of the exploits of the twentieth-century Christian writer, Dietrich Bonhoeffer, who repented from his reprehensible silence during the anti-Semitic movement of Europe and returned to his home country of Germany to face the evil of Adolf Hitler. He was eventually hung by the Gestapo for his role in the 1944 assassination attempt on Hitler. Late in his life, he wrote passionately about the role of the church to end Hitler's evil at any cost. Not only did he advocate violent action against the Nazis, he was an active participant in the planning of violence against Hitler.

Atticus affirms the ethic of protecting the powerless by allowing Heck Tate to shield Boo Radley at the novel's end. In many ways, Atticus and Heck are courageously defending Boo, a person who is as vulnerable to the town as the children were to Bob Ewell: "Mr. Finch, taking the one man who's done you and this town a great service an' draggin' him with his shy ways into the limelight—to me, that's a sin" (30). In a very real way, if the truth were told of Boo Radley's courage, it would destroy him. Atticus discusses with Heck Tate the reality of Boo's responsibility in the death of Bob Ewell, and how it would be destructive to the recluse. At the end of the chapter, he delivers the decision to Scout, who is listening to the front porch conversation. Scout tells us that her father stood silently looking at the floor for a while before looking up at her. "'Scout,' he said, 'Mr. Ewell fell on his knife. Can you possibly understand?'" (30). In an imperfect world, there are no perfect solutions. While seeking answers to the necessity of violence, it makes sense to me that an element of true courage involves protection of the powerless.

The Safest Folks in the World: Courage Is an Everyday Decision to Believe in the Resurrection

"'We're the safest folks in the world,' said Mrs. Maudie. 'We're so rarely called on to be Christians but when we are, we have men like Atticus to go for us'" (22). Maudie's words to Scout and Jem highlight some truths about the courage we observe modeled in Atticus. It is often true that our inclination is to choose safety over courage. But Scout highlights our responsibility as believers to demonstrate courage and thus to impact the world,. At the end of the novel, she recounts a scene in her elementary school classroom and shares her thoughts about Adolf Hitler and the atrocities of Nazi Germany. Scout does not understand how one man can make such horrific decisions while millions of German folks stand by and do nothing. Her childlike perspective on Hitler and the German people clarifies our dire responsibility to act as beacons of courage in an unjust world. Her commentary is an indictment of the German people for not standing up to the evils of Hitler. When I think of Dietrich Bonhoeffer, it is also an indictment of the church. In a very real sense, courage is an everyday act, and no one is held more account-able to be courageous than people of faith.

It is interesting to me that Maudie associates Atticus's courage with faith. Early in the novel, Atticus tells Scout, "I couldn't go to church and worship God if I didn't defend that man" (12). Courage is *clearly* a response of faith. As followers of Jesus, courage is the essence of our existence; not fearlessness, not front-page heroism, but the sum of all the small decisions we make each day to move the world closer to redemption. The undisputed ultimate evil, death, has been defeated in Christ, and we are called to genuinely live as though we believe that.

Yet this affirmation is the critical turning point at which the conversation about courage becomes awkward in the eyes of popular culture, at which the church stops being fashionable and becomes, instead, controversial. The foundation of true courage is unquestionably found in the resurrection of Jesus; it is the rea-son that Atticus could not worship unless he lived by his principles. To believe in courage is to understand that our actions may impact eternity with more significance than it will the right-here-and-now; the results of our courage might go unseen, unnoticed by the local papers, unheeded by our favorite Web site, even ignored by our own neighbors. As Atticus says when he is explain-ing courage to the children, "You rarely win, but sometimes you do. Mrs. Dubose won, all ninety eight pounds of her" (11). True courage is a belief that death will be defeated, and the small cou-rageous decisions we make here—day in and day out—will actually have an eternal impact. These qualities of personal responsibility, selflessness, nonviolence, and defense of the powerless are all bound in the truth of courage we learn from Atticus Finch, and thus grounded firmly in our trust of the resurrection of Jesus.

The Parable of the Missionary Tea: Our Responsibility to the Global Neighborhood Begins at Home

The whole idea of compassion is based on a keen awareness of the interdependence of all these living beings, which are all part of one another, and all involved with one another.

—Thomas Merton (1915–1968), Catholic priest, author, and activist, from a speech given the day he died

A religious man is a person who holds God and man in one thought at one time, at all times, who suffers harm done to others, whose greatest passion is compassion, whose greatest strength is love and defiance of despair.

—Abraham Heschel (1907–1972), Polish-born American rabbi and Jewish theologian

A unt Alexandra has moved into the Finch household during the trial of Tom Robinson, presumably to assist Atticus and Calpurnia with the children. Quickly she makes herself at home and begins the usual town practice of hosting missionary society meetings. Atticus makes it clear these meetings are a common expression of faith for the women of the town when he references them in a conversation with his sister, "It's just as much Maycomb County as missionary teas" (22). We are only invited into one of these meetings, and the scene constitutes a harsh and poignant indictments of racism. The missionary ladies begin by discussing the plight of a tribe from a foreign country; however, this eventually evolves into a conversation regarding their African-American neighbors whom they believe have not behaved properly since the guilty verdict in the Tom Robinson trial. The racist attitudes on display by the church people here are a vivid depiction of faith deficient of its calling to authenticity and compassion, and one of the indispensable lessons of *To Kill a Mockingbird*. This gathering of the Maycomb tribe of women who are fighting the good fight all over the living room (according to Scout) is a compelling reminder of what happens when we are afraid to be honest about our faults. It is a representation of the truth that our dishonesty about ourselves can have dangerous repercussions on the functions of the church. When we are consumed with hiding our own sins, we begin to ignore the interconnectedness of humanity, and render ourselves incapable of ministering to one another. Essentially a conversation about faith, this scene is a moving discussion of how our responsibility to the meet the needs of the global neighborhood begin at home in our own hearts.

Dressed Above Reproach:
When Fitting In Leaves Grace Out

Scout describes a scene where women are "wearing their hats" simply to cross the street. Calpurnia is dressed and starched for the primness of the party; there is an uncommon air of pretense in the Finch house for this meeting. She tells us that she is wearing her best Sunday dress, shoes, and petticoat, but is very conscious that if she spills anything on her clothes, Calpurnia might have to wash it before church the next morning. Scout is probably not the only one uncomfortable with having to wear her Sunday attire to this Saturday event, but she is certainly the only one who recognizes it. The older women are dressed in their finest clothes for a very formal afternoon.

But like many *religious* practices, this gathering performed in the name of God is profoundly lacking the qualities of grace and love that should be synonymous with His commands. Scout identifies something very disingenuous about how these women are presenting themselves to each other when she acknowledges the inconvenience to her beloved housekeeper. She is very considerate and mindful of the fact that if she is not careful, she may create more work for Calpurnia, who, like any good mother, would have to wash and prepare Scout's attire for church the next day. Because of her color, though, it is unlikely that any of the other attendees of the function would share the same consideration for Calpurnia.

On the surface, there is something innocent and Southern about the tradition of dressing up for a religious function; however, there is also an element of danger about its intent implied in this scene. Even the conversation between the women is dressed up, civilized, correct, and distrustful. Scout inadvertently points out the hazard of this external propriety when she recounts the women who are in attendance. "It was customary for every circle hostess to invite her neighbors in for refreshments, be they Baptists or Presbyterians, which accounted for the presence of Miss Rachel (sober as a judge), Miss Maudie and Miss Stephanie Crawford" (24). Miss Rachel Haverford is a closet drinker, and her presence "sober as a judge" is an affirmation that these women are cautious to put their best foot forward in each other's presence. A gathering done in the name of a faith that tells us to come as we are—the true spirit of meeting in the name of Christ—is hardly present here. For many of us, like the women of the tea, the practice of faith is a measure of how well we can hide our own sin.

My brother and I can recount with great angst the ordeal of getting dressed to attend church services. We both laugh about it and vividly remember the discomfort of the three-piece navy suits we were forced to wear for one particular Easter service, complete with red carnations. On the surface , there is nothing inherently bad about the formality of religious practice. My Grandmother Litton always dressed up and prepared an extravagantly beautiful

Sunday lunch for after church. But her intent was to honor the Sabbath. Her transparency with the church and her community made it clear that "dressing up" was her effort to celebrate togetherness and family.

I thought about my childhood church attire the other day, as I threw on an old T-shirt and headed out the door to a service; the formality of a suit has been replaced by a trendy T-shirt and jeans in some areas of the world. In some religious tribes, "propriety" has been supplanted by "cool" when it comes to the fashion of dressing for church. And that's fine. But it is the spirit of putting on airs (such as what happens at the missionary tea) that is dangerous. It is problematic when cosmetic dressing up has the clear intention of hiding our imperfections. Whether we are dressed down with tattoos showing for a gathering at Mosiac in Los Angeles or dressed up in our finest suit for a service at First Baptist Church in Atlanta, we must always make sure that we are not masking the condition of our hearts with language and attire, lest our faith become a show and church just another social club. There is a quote often attributed to writer Brennan Manning in which he says there is a beautiful transparency to honest disciples who never wear a false face and do not pretend to be anything but who they are—and this cuts skillfully to the core of the missionary circle's dilemma. The pretending that takes place at the meeting is nothing new to religious practice.

It has been part of religious culture since the time of Jesus to put our best foot forward and hide our weaknesses and faults. Jesus responds to this practice by the church folks of His day saying, "Woe to you, teachers of the law and Pharisees, you hypocrites!

You clean the outside of the cup and dish, but inside they are full of greed and self-indulgence . . . on the outside you appear to people as righteous, but inside you are full of hypocrisy and wickedness" (Matthew 23:25, 28, NIV). He was talking about using God as a practice, rather than a faith, saying we should be cognizant of the One who sees beyond our latest devout and righteous-looking appearance. When hiding ourselves behind religiosity becomes the order of the day, grace is left by the wayside; without being honest about our own sin, we will never show compassion toward others. If we are to adorn ourselves with anything, it should be with compassion and honesty—the foundations of connecting to our community.

Scout tells us, "Today Aunt Alexandra and her missionary circle were fighting the good fight all over the house" (24). This line, delivered tongue-in-cheek, is a clear reference to Paul's letter to Timothy. It is an oft-quoted scripture; Paul tells Timothy, "Fight the good fight of the faith. Take hold of the eternal life to which you were called when you made your good confession in the presence of many witnesses" (1 Tim. 6:12, NIV). Scout's sarcastic reference to this famous verse makes it clear: while the meeting is being done in the name of faith, the true spirit of the "good fight" is exactly what is missing from the scene. The ladies at the meeting are busy hiding behind religious language. Absent from the Missionary Tea is Paul's prerequisite for that good fight: the good confession. It is by recognizing and confessing our own sin that we acknowledge the overwhelming element of God's grace extended to us. We often spurn confession and grace in favor of hiding ourselves in nice clothes, adorning ourselves with gossip, or masking our deficiencies behind the faults of others. Like the Maycomb women, we can't practice compassion for those beyond our own tribe when we are too busy running from grace. Transparency and compassion are missing from the Missionary Circle.

The "Poor" Mrunas: Pity Is Part of Dressing Up

Scout is able to overhear most of the conversation about the Mrunas from the kitchen, where she is helping Aunt Alexandra and Calpurnia prepare and serve refreshments. She recounts, "I heard Mrs. Grace Merriweather giving a report on the squalid lives of the Mrunas" (24). When she joins the group of women in the living room, she engages Mrs. Merriweather by asking what the women studied. "'Oh, child, those poor Mrunas,' she said, and was off" (24). Mrs. Merriweather exhibits in her tone that the women are discussing the Mrunas with an air of condescension. By calling them poor she is demonstrating a sense of superiority. She calls the Mrunas squalid, meaning insanitary, unpleasant, lacking in dignity and moral value.

This is religion at its worst. The ladies discuss the Mrunas not with compassion, but with self-righteous pity. Displaying pity seems an integral practice at this religious event—it is as essential to them as maintaining their appearance of piety. I believe pity is a staple of religion rather than faith. Pity is much different from compassion; to pity someone is to disdain them. Pity has no reverence for the animate character of other human beings; it allows the women to ignore the humanness of this group called the Mrunas. It is not respectful and it is not a response of love.

As a young teenager I traveled on a mission trip to Peru with a very self-righteous understanding that I would have pity on what I would find there. Instead, I remember being completely taken aback at the vibrancy of the Christians we met there. In the face of hardships, they lived out their faith with an authentic compassion and love I had never seen before. I realized that maybe those people we had come to minister to would end up ministering to us about the realities of faith. In retrospect, I often wonder if believers around the world don't pity us in our religious piety and lack of priorities. The members of the communities in Peru loved each other with such deep compassion that it was natural for them to reach out to others and to us with the same grace. In fact, I am not sure they even viewed us as "others."

Pity is an emotion that empowers us to continue pretending we do not need God's grace. Compassion, absent from Aunt Alexandra's Missionary Tea, is a much different response. While pity shows a lack of respect for other human beings, compassion has its roots in a deep respect for others. Pity is an emotion; compassion is a connection. Compassion sees the Other as equal. Compassion happens when we care for another person enough to make his problems our own. It is no wonder compassion is difficult for people who are too busy trying to hide their own sins so they will be accepted into the social club of religion. Mrs. Merriweather and the rest of the Missionary Tea pity or objectify the Mrunas in order to make themselves feel better, to improve their own sense of security, and, ultimately to view themselves justified before God.

Us Versus Them: Mruna Culture and Maycomb Culture

I remember as a young child sitting in Sunday night church services and watching mission videos. Many of them were moving stories of the wonderful things that God seemed to be doing in distant lands. I guess most of us who grow up in that type of setting feel as though the missionaries are taking God to the land they are visiting. It never occurred to me until my experience in Peru that *God was already there*. It is funny how we religious folks believe in an omnipresent God, but kind of hang it on ourselves to take Him places. If anything really happened for me on the mission field, it was that I saw God operating in more vivid and extravagant ways than I had ever seen. It allowed me to see through different lenses how He might be working back home in my own first-world suburban life, school, and family.

This lack of understanding the cultural differences between the Maycomb clan and the Mrunas is devoid of the compassion of God. As Scout recounts, "They put the women out in huts when their time came, whatever that was; they had no sense of family— I knew that'd distress Aunty— . . . they were crawling with yaws and earworms, they chewed up and spat out the bark of a tree into a communal pot and then got drunk on it" (24). While the getting drunk part must have sounded secretly appealing to a closet alcoholic like Miss Rachel, the social traditions of this tribe of Mrunas are discussed with scorn by the Maycomb tribe of ladies. I always wonder how hilarious it might be to hear a Mruna who had visited the Maycomb religious gathering report back to his own tribe about the strange habits of the white Alabama folks, with all their makeup, insincerity, dainty little snacks, and feigned sobriety. These ladies aren't tolerant of the Mruna culture. They do not recognize the humanity of the Mrunas, and therefore, really aren't as concerned with bringing the message of Jesus to these people as much as they are in indoctrinating them into civilized culture. This is always the result of religion practiced without compassion, and in words often attributed to Francis Schaeffer, "Biblical orthodoxy [practicing religion] without compassion is surely the ugliest thing in the world."

Go back through the history of the church and you will find stories of absolute intolerance for those perceived as uncivilized. I have read histories from the nineteenth century of Native American Indian boys being beaten for continuing to observe their own traditions instead of the "Christian" practices of their educators. We can even look all the way back to Pope Gregory's treatment of the Anglo-Saxons. My brother, an English professor, wrote a paper titled "Unfamiliar Blood" in which he recounted the pope's disdain for the practices of the people he was converting. While it should be noted that Gregory is responsible for the preservation of Western culture in many wonderful ways, I think his well-intentioned efforts also destroyed a little of the beauty of Anglo-Saxon culture in his attempt to convert the inhabitants of Britain to a Roman expression of Christianity he deemed more palatable.

This is the lack of connection, the lack of compassion, which leads us to convert other cultures to our comfortable practices rather than trusting the faith in Christ to grow in the fertile roots of their own civilization. I have read accounts of how richly, beautifully, and differently the practice of the Christian faith is lived out in parts of South America. My friends who are missionaries around the world are knocked out by the richness of the celebration, the vibrancy and beauty of faith that grows out of other cultures and traditions. The irony of this scene is that the "civilized" cultural practices of the Maycomb tea could be perceived as uncivilized in the very culture they pity. The Missionary Circle is comprised of a group of religious folk who are barely tolerant of their own differences; they will hardly accept them in the Mrunas.

Jesus Never Went Around Complaining:
True Compassion Begins At Home

We can't begin to speak of compassion for people across the world until we can show the fortitude to love the people in our own neighborhood. The Missionary Tea takes an even more wretched turn when the women discuss the African-American community of Maycomb. Mrs. Merriweather transitions from her conversation about the Mrunas to Tom Robinson's wife and children without stopping to take a breath, but Scout understands what she is saying.

"'Thing that church ought to do is help her lead a Christian life . . . Some of the men ought to go out there and tell that preacher to encourage her" (24). It is clearly implied in these lines that these women wouldn't dream of personally interacting with the black community in Maycomb. The dialogue degenerates into something even more racist and devoid of understanding when the ladies chime in to discuss how their black servants have been "sulking" since the verdict of Tom's case. The outrageousness of the discourse is heightened with Mrs. Merriweather's commentary on her African-American housekeeper's "unchristian" behavior: "You know what I said to my Sophy, Gertrude? 'Jesus never went around grumbling and complaining,' and you know, it did her good'" (24). Mrs. Merriweather is referencing her housekeeper, a member of a community devastated at the injustice leveled by white jury against Tom Robinson. Could there be anything more contemptible than oppressing a group of people and then commanding them to act like Jesus in response to the injustice? Jesus never rejected anyone because of his or her race, culture, social class, or even gender. In the Hebrew culture, it was taboo to interact with others outside of the Jewish community, yet Jesus healed a Roman servant, preached about compassion for Samaritans, and interacted with anyone in need who crossed His path.

For those on the outside who view themselves as separate from the church, this scene clearly demonstrates the hypocrisy of these Christian women who are voicing concern for the Mrunas while demonstrating indifference for their oppressed black neighbors. Mrs. Merriweather's lines simply turn my stomach—they are disgusting. But the sad reality for people of faith who read these lines is found in the realization that there actually is no hypocrisy. There is a consistent disregard for the connectedness of humanity, beginning with the participants in the room, extending to their African-American neighbors, and reaching across the globe to the "poor" Mrunas! It is a symptom of their religion, which is devoid of compassion. The ladies demonstrate nothing but contempt for the oppressed—whether they are ten thousand miles away or just down the street in Maycomb. Fortunately, our heroine, Mrs. Maudie, finally loses patience with the injustice of the conversation and curtly shuts it down with some terse remarks to Miss Merriweather. But the lack of compassion is exposed and the sins of Maycomb are far-reaching.

The Saintly J. Grimes Everett: Send Someone for the Poor Mrunas

"Mrs. Merriweather's large brown eyes always filled with tears when she considered the oppressed. 'Not a white person'll go near 'em but that saintly J. Grimes Everett'" (24). As Mrs. Merriweather discusses the Mrunas, the interconnectedness of humanity becomes very clear. The link between the sinfulness and pity of the women in Maycomb toward the Mrunas is founded in their intolerance for one another and racist pity for their neighbors. Mrs. Merriweather attributes J. Grimes Everett's holiness to the color of his skin— his appearance. I wonder if there might be a divide between his work and her understanding of it. J. Grimes Everett, a man we know little about, has actually put himself in the field and is, at least, dedicated to forming a connection with the Mrunas. He is an ornament being used by the women of the Missionary Tea to cloak themselves in righteousness. He is their protection from real compassion. "Mrs. Merriweather played her voice like an organ; every word she said received its full measure: 'The poverty . . . the darkness . . . the immorality—nobody but J. Grimes Everett knows... J. Grimes Everett said to me, he said, "Mrs. Merriweather, you have no conception, no conception of what we are fighting over there.""" (24).

I always wonder if poor J. Grimes Everett had any idea how he was enabling Mrs. Merriweather to be the star of the missionary tea. She is a woman who, we are told, really doesn't even exhibit compassion to her own husband. I'd like to think that if Mr. Everett had any idea he was helping facilitate their lack of compassion he might quit his mission work and come to Maycomb to witness to the missionary circle and clear up their misunderstandings of the gospel.

Mrs. Merriweather continues her tear-filled diatribe about the Poor Mrunas. "'Mr. Everett,' I said, 'the ladies of the Maycomb Alabama Methodist Episcopal Church are behind you one hundred percent . . . I said to myself, when I go home I'm going to give a course on the Mrunas and bring J. Grimes Everett's message to Maycomb'" (24). While the real work is being done by Mr. Everett, Mrs. Merriweather holds herself up for the adulation of the other women of the meeting as the one responsible for taking part in his mission. How? By sitting in the comfortable living room full of broken relationships and "bringing" his message to Maycomb. The hypocrisy of her words is overwhelming. The women have convinced themselves they are doing something spiritual, something that equals the work of Mr. Everett, by dressing up and having tea over their discussion of the oppressed and unfortunate people to whom he ministers. It brings to mind the controversial verse in the book of James, "In the same way, faith by itself, if it is not accompanied by action, is dead" (2:17, NIV). Maybe the lesson we should take from J. Grimes Everett is that true compassion requires action.

We are blessed to attend a church that endeavors to care for people. Hundreds of parishioners crowded in the sanctuary on a recent Saturday to work towards that goal. The chairs were put away, stations were set up, and for hours people worked diligently to pack rice and nonperishables into food packets that could be shipped to Haiti. Our church's response to this challenge was inspiring: in a day of work, we were able to put together enough packets of food to feed thousands of Haitian children. Was this true compassion? Yes. We weren't face-to-face with those people, experiencing their plight with them. Rather, we were empowered through our connections to each other and the honesty with which we practice community. This connection to the far away land was born out of our diligence in daily practicing compassion locally. The seeds planted by caring for each other and tending to our own neighborhood grew into vines of love and compassion that were able to reach all the way to Haiti. Compassion happens when people of faith are honest with each other, when they put aside their need to dress themselves above reproach, and when transparency frees them to care for others. Connecting with humanity on our own turf leads to a connection with humanity across the world. And there is a desperate need for that type of compassion from the American church.

When I think about the lines of J. Grimes Everett to Mrs. Merriweather, I am struck with the truths of his statement, "You have no conception, no conception of what we are fighting over there" (24). Many of us do not have a conception of the challenges present in the global neighborhood. But once we have that awareness, we become accountable. The practice of compassion in our churches and neighborhoods must grow into compassion for our brothers and sisters around the world. There are grave needs awaiting our response. The ministry Blood:Water Mission began funding a late-stage AIDS hospice and discovered the vital link between living with HIV/AIDS and the need for clean water. As a result, they launched the 1000 Wells Project in 2005, a nationwide effort to raise enough money to provide clean water and sanitation to one thousand communities in sub-Saharan Africa, based on the humbling reality that one dollar will provide one African with clean water for an entire year. The Red Campaign founded by Bono has helped a substantial number of children in Africa who have suffered at the hands of AIDS. In our own hemisphere, undernourishment affects fifty-four million people; Haiti, El Salvador, Guatemala, Honduras, Nicaragua, Argentina, Colombia, and Peru, are confronting grave hunger situations today. Freedom from Hunger tells us that 53 percent of Mexico's population is living on less than two dollars per day, while close to 24 percent are living on less than one dollar per day. The organization calls these families "food-insecure," meaning they cannot meet even their most basic nutritional needs for most of the year. And according to the International Food Policy Research Institute, Southeast Asia has been identified as the region that has the highest levels of child malnutrition in the world.

The harsh reality of our impotence as people of faith is vividly reflected in the needs of our neighbors across the globe, which are staggering. The lesson we learn attending the Missionary Tea originates in the very nature of the gathering. Until we are truthful with one another, transparent about our faults, and begin to reach out to each other with the grace extended to us by God, we will not experience compassion that requires us to attend to the suffering of the world. Compassion must begin at home, in our hearts, with candid confessions to each other of our dire need for God. It begins with the acceptance of those closest to us. Once compassion is planted and begins to grow, it will not stop. It will empower us to reach out first to our own neighborhoods and then to the world. Our responsibility to the global community begins when we stop viewing members of humanity as "others," when we are enabled through our own transparency to connect with the world through the eyes of those in need. At some point we must stop talking, abandon the energy of dressing up our own sins, stop having Missionary

Teas, and walk out our front doors to engage the needs of the local and world community. At some point, we have to realize the interconnectedness of humanity and respond to the dire circumstances of the less fortunate across the globe.

The Parable of the Great Depression: The Christian Ethic of Financial Responsibility

Financial peace isn't the acquisition of stuff. It is learning to live on less than you make, so you can give money back.

—DAVE RAMSEY (B. 1960), AMERICAN AUTHOR, FROM *FINANCIAL PEACE*

Don't matter how much money you got, there's only two kinds of people: there's saved people and there's lost people.

—BOB DYLAN (B. 1941), AT A SHOW IN 1979 IN TEMPE, AZ
(QUOTED IN *BOB DYLAN: BEHIND THE SHADES REVISITED*)

S cout Finch explains the ethics of Maycomb's children after she and her brother Jem discover two Indian head coins. "Finders were keepers unless a title was proven . . . helping ourselves to someone's scuppernongs was part of ethical culture, but money was different" (4). The kids decide it is prudent to question the children at school and make certain the coins are not someone else's property. Even at a young age they understand the significance of money.

I listened to Pastor Andy Stanley say to his congregation once that if you truly want to determine what you value, how you order your life, and what constitutes the priorities of your heart, it is as simple as taking the time to examine your financial statements. Since then, my wife and I have periodically sat down together and looked at our checking account to reaffirm our principles as a family; we have shuddered on occasion to discover what was reflected there.

We live in a world that values the dollar and what we believe it can bring us above all else. We are a society driven by a longing for the material, in which the dollar is too often valued higher on the exchange than human relationships. We all seem a little too consumed at times with keeping up, and with the sense that we are not going to get what we deserve. We are discontented and often believe that what we can earn, acquire, wear, or drive, will finally deliver the joy and satisfaction we long for. The Bible teaches us something quite different: "For we brought nothing into the world, and we can take nothing out of it. But if we have food and clothing, we will be content with that. People who want to get rich fall into temptation and a trap and into many foolish and harmful desires that plunge men into ruin and destruction. For the love of money is a root of all kinds of evil. Some people, eager for money, have wandered from the faith and pierced themselves with many griefs" (1 Timothy 6:7–10, NIV). A visit to Maycomb allows us to peek back in time, behind the curtain of the Great Depression; to examine a people who learned the necessity living by different set of financial ethics and principles.

Nowhere To Go and Nothing To Buy: A Culture of Consumerism and Unrest

In the opening lines of the novel, Scout describes to us a world much different than ours today: "There was no hurry, for there was nowhere to go, nothing to buy and no money to buy it with, nothing to see outside the boundaries of Maycomb County" (1). One of the most compelling aspects about the setting of *To Kill a Mockingbird* is that it unfolds during the years of the Great Depression. The economy is part of the landscape on which the novel is painted; the attitudes and disciplines that were common practice in the1930s seem eerily relevant to our situation in twenty-first–century America. To the readers of Lee's novel in the 1960s, these succinct and finely articulated lines were probably a sobering reminder of the hardships of the Depression, but for readers today and future generations of readers, I imagine two phrases gleam like indistinct neon signs on a foggy highway. "No hurry" and "nothing to buy" imply a culture not driven by consumerism and not captivated, as the current culture is, by the hectic rush to position ourselves for another purchase that we believe will equate to happiness. One of my favorite authors and speakers talks about employing the wisdom of our great grandparents in dealing with today's financial decisions; this is a theme reflected in the setting and diction of our story.

But the backdrop for the novel also points to another aspect of Maycomb life that reminds me of the powerful words of psychiatrist and philosopher Carl Jung, who once said, "Hurry is not *of* the Devil; it *is* the Devil."[1] There is something implicit in our feverish consumption that keeps us moving at breakneck pace. I know from personal experience that we can become so consumed with what we think we need that we completely lose sight of the realities around us that make our lives rich. There is very little room left to "be still and know that I am God" (see Ps. 46:10) under the bright lights and blaring noise of advertising. There were harsh realities to the Great Depression that I clearly remember recounted in my grandparents' stories. However, I believe that we can examine the values of that time without romanticizing a period of bitter hardships for those who lived through it, including the good people of Maycomb.

Scout continues to set the scene for the novel: "But there was a vague optimism for some people; Maycomb County had recently been told that it had nothing to fear but fear itself" (1). Scout is invoking the timely words of the president of the United States. These lines, which are so pivotal to the setting of the novel, would have been a disheartening reminder of the Great Depression to mature readers in the 1950s and '60s. Spoken in 1933 by a newly elected president who, according to many historians, had said as little as he could during the campaign about what he would actually do if elected, these words echoed in the novel reflect the impact the inaugural address of President Franklin D. Roosevelt had on the citizens of Maycomb County (and the citizens of the United States), although their has been completely glossed over by the passage of time. It sent me searching for the complete lines of FDR's famous speech, and I was inspired by the profundity of what I found in his words: "Happiness lies not in the mere possession of money; it lies in the joy of achievement, in the thrill of creative effort. The joy and moral stimulation of work no longer must be forgotten in the mad chase of evanescent profits. These dark days will be worth all they cost us if they teach us that our true destiny is not to be ministered unto but to minister to ourselves and to our fellow men. Recognition of the falsity of material wealth as the standard of success goes hand in hand with the abandonment of the false belief that public office and high political position are to be valued only by the standards of pride of place and personal profit."[2] This address is worth mentioning because it was a deep reminder to the people of Maycomb that their common difficulties were only material. The elements of the setting of *To Kill a Mockingbird* should remind us that we are born into a culture that at one time was able to come to terms with the meaningful realities of life. There are truths embedded in the background of the novel: there is a morality to work, to money, to finances; and consumerism and debt should never cloud the eternal calling that we are ultimately responsible for each other.

"No Church Baskets and No Scrip Stamps": We Can't Change the World as Slaves to Debt

Scout Finch is not happy about her first day at school. She is given position of class spokesperson by her first grade teacher—the young and inexperienced Ms. Caroline Fisher—who demonstrates no knowledge or frame of reference for dealing with Maycomb culture. When Ms. Fisher realizes that Scout's classmate Walter Cunningham has no lunch, she offers to give him lunch money. Walter quietly refuses and it is left up to Scout to explain the Cunningham family philosophy to her teacher. Later in the narrative, Scout tells us Walter's people have a reputation around Maycomb County as a family who never take anything they cannot pay back. Although they have been hit very hard by the Depression, the Cunninghams live by a set of principles that Scout describes at length. "They get along on what they have. They don't have much but they get along on it" (2) We learn later that Mr. Cunningham's land is tied up in some sort of "entailment," which apparently is an old-fashioned way of saying someone had imparted land to the family in a will and its legal ownership was under litigation. Atticus seems to respect this man's ethics. He tells Scout that Mr. Cunningham came from a "set breed of men" (2). The Cunningham family's practices, as described by Scout, constitute a responsibility that is completely foreign to today's culture. Mr. Cunningham, who has his own financial problems, is viewed as someone who will not borrow what he cannot pay back. This cultural idea was common in the 1930s but seems lost on us today, in which debt is truly a form of poverty.

I read recently that the average American household has seven credit cards. In 2009, the average credit card debt per household was over $16,000. A recent study estimated the debt of the average household in our country to be well over $121, 958. If we were to include federal debt in that calculation, it would tally over $668,000 per family. Couple these figures with the fact that the average income in America totals close to $43,000 per year, the debt figures appear catastrophic. In Greek culture, financial debt was tied to actual physical bondage. In other words, if one was unable to pay his debt, one actually became the property of his lender. I wonder if this idea is not still devastatingly true in many ways. The Hebrews were called to observe strict guidelines concerning debt; Deuteronomy 15:8 and 28:12 are both very clear in their admonitions against borrowing. The wisdom of Proverbs implores its readers, "The rich rule over the poor, and the borrower is servant to the lender" (22:7, NIV). Debt is slavery—and not just physical slavery but spiritual and emotional slavery.

There is a spiritual element to the twenty-first–century problem of debt. Paul's letter to the Philippians articulates our spiritual deficiency when he writes, ". . . for I have learned to be content whatever the circumstances. I know what it is to be in need, and I know what it is to have plenty. I have learned the secret of being content in any and every situation, whether well fed or hungry, whether living in plenty or in want. I can do everything through him who gives me strength." (Phil. 4:11–13, NIV).

There is a contentment and a resolve found in the Cunninghams and the people of Maycomb that is absent in today's culture. The Cunninghams, who receive help from Atticus to work through their entailment, will not accept what they cannot afford to pay back. Scout asks her father if the Mr. Cunningham will pay him back. "'Not in money,' Atticus said, 'but before the year's out I'll have been paid.' . . . One morning Jem and I found a load of stove-wood in the back yard . . . With Christmas came a crate of smilax and holly. That spring when we found a crokersack full of turnip greens, Atticus said Mr. Cunningham had more than paid him" (2). The contrasts between the attitudes of the people of Maycomb and our practices seem almost an insurmountable divide. I think that financial guru Dave Ramsey articulates it beautifully when he says, "Debt has been sold to us so aggressively, so loudly, and so often that to imagine living without debt requires myth-busting . . . Debt is so ingrained into our culture that most Americans can't even envision a car without a payment, a house without a mortgage, a student without a loan, and credit without a card. We have been sold debt with such repetition and such fervor that most folks cannot conceive what it would be like to have no payments."[3] Debt is so pervasive that we are barely able to use our resources for good. We are part of a culture in dire need of rediscovering the ethics and principals of swearing off debt that led Atticus to reverently describe Mr. Cunningham as coming from "a set breed of men."

Doctors, Lawyers, and . . . Valuing People Over the Dollar

As Scout discusses the plight of the Cunninghams with Atticus, we learn more about the financial situations of the families of Maycomb during the Great Depression. When Scout asks her father if the family is as poor as the Cunninghams, he responds that the depression had been hardest on the country people— farmers especially. Atticus tells Scout that the poverty of the farmers affects the whole economy, explaining, "As Maycomb County was farm country, nickels and dimes were hard to come by for doctors and dentists and lawyers" (2). The beauty of what Scout is learning in this discussion is that Atticus values people over what they can give him. He is aware that the Cunninghams are unable to pay, and yet he still feels morally obligated to offer them his services. Atticus is not the only professional who does this sort of thing for the struggling people of Maycomb.

Atticus is practicing another ethic that has been left behind in today's culture of voracious consumerism. He does not equate the status of his neighbors with how they can benefit him financially. It is obvious that Atticus does not choose to defend the innocent Tom Robinson (thus raising the ire of the town against his family) for financial gain. He takes the case because it is the right thing to do. He tells Scout at one point, "If I didn't defend that man I couldn't go to church and worship God" (2). He is acutely aware of his spiritual obligation to love and care for his neighbor.

The gospel repeatedly discusses the value of people in relation to money, from Jesus' observation of the poor widow giving the little that she has, to His interaction with the rich man who wants to join the disciples. The most poignant commentary on the handling of wealth is found in Luke 3:11, when John the Baptist says: "The man with two tunics should share with him who has none, and the one who has food should do the same" (NIV). The Bible consistently preaches the value of relationships over money; Jesus calls for a moral equity in caring for other human beings that we often do not practice in our culture.

I read recently that only 8 percent of people in the world own a car, yet the average American household owns between two and three. Close to 800 million people in the world will not eat today; 300 million of them are children. It is estimated that Americans and Europeans spend close to $400 billion each year . . . going out to dinner. Over one billion people in the world today live on one dollar a day, yet last year Americans spent over $33 billion . . . on weight-loss products. Americans are also by far the most giving people on the planet, but these figures serve as an illustration that we need to realign our values when it pertains to money. When we consider the level of human suffering in the world that could be wiped away with the application of our disposable resources, we should pause and reflect on the words of Jesus. It makes me wonder if we cannot afford to be more like Atticus in our principles. Sometimes we are so immersed in our crusade to consume, so overtaken with what we are convinced we need to make us happy that we are too distracted to grasp the spiritual responsibility of our wealth. I think the answer to the dilemma begins with valuing people over materials and wealth. It also a discipline that calls us to daily practice, to ordering our existence around the call to follow the One who is the greatest giver to ever live.

Collection for Tom and a Surprise Breakfast: Giving Is Essential to Our Faith

Two of the most moving scenes for me in *To Kill a Mockingbird* involve beautiful acts of giving. The first occurs on Jem and Scout's visit to the African-American church with Calpurnia. Tom Robinson, whose wife and children attend First Purchase Church, is in jail and unable to care for his family. The pastor of the congregation closes the doors to the church in a dramatic scene and asks the congregation to give enough money to get the Robinson family through the week. After the church service, Scout curiously asks Reverend Sykes why they are giving offering money to Helen Robinson. "'Didn't you hear why?' asked Reverend Sykes. 'Helen's got three little 'uns and she can't go out to work'" (12). This scene is special for me because I have always felt like it is simply the picture of the church doing its job. I wonder what could happen if the church-with-a-capital-C—that is, all of us—responded the same way. The theologian Walter Brueggeman speaks about our response to this calling with brutal honesty: "The contemporary American church is so largely enculturated to the American ethos of consumerism that it has little power to believe or to act."[4] His words are powerful. Are we so set on what we want that we are completely oblivious to the real needs of others?

The second scene that brings me almost to tears takes place after Atticus has lost the Tom Robinson trial. The Finch family wakes up one morning to quite a surprise. Calpurnia tells Atticus that Tom Robinson's father has given them a chicken for breakfast, to which Atticus replies that even the president probably doesn't have chicken for breakfast. As he begins to notice the unusually extravagant morning fare, Calpurnia tells him that he should step into the kitchen to look for himself. Scout tells us, "The kitchen table was loaded with enough food to bury the family: hunks of salt pork, tomatoes, beans . . . Calpurnia said, 'This was all over 'round the back steps when I got here this morning. They—they 'preciate what you did, Mr. Finch.' Atticus's eyes filled with tears. He did not speak a moment. 'Tell them I am very grateful,' he said. 'Tell them—tell them they must never do this again. Times are too hard'" (22). There is a beautiful reality found in both of these pictures of benevolence. The gifts are presented by people who are poor and have little to offer. Atticus tears up in this scene when he realizes the significance of the gifts he has been given and the substantial cost for the givers. It is the only instance in the entire novel where Scout notices her father's tears. It calls to mind the gospel account of Jesus and his disciples as they observe a poor widow. "Sitting across from the offering box, [Jesus] was observing how the crowd tossed money in for the collection. Many of the rich were making large contributions. One poor widow came up and put in two small coins—a measly two cents. Jesus called his disciples over and, 'The truth is that this poor widow gave more to the collection than all the others put together. All the others gave what they'll never miss; she gave extravagantly what she couldn't afford—she gave her all'" (Mark 12:41–43, MSG). Jesus is practicing His customary discipline of tearing down the letter of the law and bringing the spirit of it to the attention of His followers. It is not what we give—it is how we give. I referenced earlier that Americans give 306 billion a year to charity. While America gives more money to charity than any country in the world, the percentage of that giving compared to average income is not very high; our total giving, as a nation, is just above 2 percent. This is a far cry from the practice of 10 percent that originated in the Valley of the Kings in the book of Genesis and has remained a constant in the Judeo-Christian tradition. Jesus is makes it clear to His disciples during this observation of the poor woman: to those who have much, much is required (see Luke 12:48).

It is dangerous when preachers misrepresent the rewards of giving as being financial ones. There is an ethos too often referenced in sermons: if you give so much, God will give it back—and the inference is always "in dollars." Some are brazen enough to say that God will fatten your bank account if you give. There is a richness found in intentional giving, but it is not financial success. We were challenged last Christmas as a family to try to consume less and give more during the holidays. The very small sacrifices we made, our intentionality of giving up some items that we thought we wanted in order to help those who were really in need, made it one of the best family Christmases we have ever experienced. It left us hungry to give more.

There is a deep sense of fulfillment found when we share our "two tunics" with the family who has none. It is partially the affirmation to the other person that we care about his needs—a connection to him as a human being. But giving also vacates an area of our soul to be inhabited by the eternal richness, a wealth that is only discovered by dethroning consumerism—our incessant desire for a piece of the pie.

Is there a financial benefit in giving? Of course there is, and it is found in the fact that if we begin intentionally giving, we must learn to pay closer attention to our bank account. We begin to look at what we spend and where, we begin to notice that our hearts are reflected in the direction of our dollars. The most beautiful aspect of the offering by the African-American community in these scenes of *To Kill a Mockingbird* is the spirit with which the giving is performed. They demonstrate a deep sense of personal responsibility and respect for their neighbors. If we are to give as God would have us give, these attitudes should reflect the bent of our hearts. I read a moving quote by the lead singer and activist Bono recently: "Americans, Irish people, are good at charity. We like to give, and we give a lot, even those who can't afford it. But justice is a higher standard." When Bono speaks of justice, I believe he is pointing to a lofty goal. Quite honestly, I believe that as followers of God, we are called to an even higher standard than justice. We are called to the ethic of giving that Jesus modeled—an ideal of compassion. It is after all, true compassion that leads to the gratefulness shown in the giving to Atticus and to the Robinson family. True compassion is modeled in Atticus's and Dr. Reynold's efforts to help the people of

Maycomb. The Proverbs tell us that "the righteous gives and does not hold back" (21:26, NASB).

Nothing Left of Miss Maudie's House:
A Return to the Wisdom of Our Great Grandparents

One of the memorable events of the novel takes place when a fire breaks out on the Finches' street and Mrs. Maudie, watches helplessly as the flames devour her home. It appears that Maudie has lost everything. Imagine waking to find that the sum total of everything we accumulated in our lives was completely gone: every material possession, every shred of wealth. Let's place ourselves in Maudie's skin for a moment; how would we really respond to such misfortune? The morning after the fire, the children are returning her sun hat and hedge clippers (very few of her possessions were rescued from the flames) and surveying the devastation of the night before. "Miss Maudie looked around, and the shadow of her old grin crossed her face. 'Always wanted a smaller house, Jem Finch.' . . .'You ain't grievin', Miss. Maudie?' I asked, surprised. Atticus said her house was nearly all she had" (8). Maudie's resilience is a vivid reflection of her priorities and where she invests her trust. There is nothing wrong with material wealth and accumulation, as long as it doesn't consume our lives.

I don't know if the attitudes toward money and material possessions are an intentional theme of the novel; it may be simply the common sense of the time period in which it is set. But again and again, we experience characters who value people more than dollars and relationships over possessions. If we could really fix our focus on ministering to each other, if we really valued what makes us rich, I wonder how it could transform our lives—and transform the world. Jesus says, "So do not worry, saying, 'What shall we eat?' or 'What shall we drink?' or 'What shall we wear?' For the pagans [read: nonbelievers] run after all these things, and your heavenly Father knows that you need them" (Matt. 6:31–32, NIV).

The people of Maycomb have looked squarely in the face of complete financial loss. Many have been shown how quickly all of the material wealth and security they worked for could vanish in the Great Depression. They have confronted economic insecurity and know its place in their lives. However, the meaningful aspects of life go on. Miss Maudie's shrugging off the possible devastation of losing all she owned is a wonderful lesson of life's abundance if we can simply realign our priorities. I vaguely remember the economic hardships of the 1970s; I was a young child at the time. But I remember the recession of the early 1990s, the economic trials after 9/11, and am certainly cognizant of the economic challenges we face in this century. It reminds me of a favorite Ralph Waldo Emerson quote: "Can anyone remember when times were not hard and money not scarce?" Economic challenges are, of course, very real. But if we have our values in the right place, if we trust in the eternal, if we place our investments in people, then we will not be harmed by the comings and goings of wealth. If we can learn to view money not as our own, but as a gift from our heavenly

Father, maybe we can walk away from consumerism and stay out of debt. We may actually have the freedom to change the world with our giving. The wisdom of our great-grandparents calls us to values we desperately need today.

The Parable of Tom Robinson: How Compassion Can Overcome Our Differences

Let us all hope that the dark clouds of racial prejudice will soon pass away, and that in some not too distant tomorrow the radiant stars of love and brotherhood will shine over our great nation with all their scintillating beauty.

—Rev Martin Luther King Jr. (1929–1968),
Letter from Birmingham Jail, 16 April 1963

I believe in the Kingdom Come, Then all the colours will bleed into one . . .

—Bono (b. 1960), lyrics to "Where the Streets Have No Name"
(U2: *The Joshua Tree*)

Thesе lines are spoken by Atticus to his brother, Jack, as they discuss the upcoming trial of Tom Robinson, an innocent black man accused of rape: "I hope and pray that I can get Jem and Scout through it without bitterness, and most of all, without catching Maycomb's usual disease" (9). It is one of Atticus's many lines about the evil that pervades the daily life of his town. In many ways, Harper Lee's beloved novel *is* the parable of Tom Robinson: he is the undeniable centerpiece of the most enduring and important theme of *To Kill a Mockingbird*. We are now cognizant of the oppressive racial prejudice that permeated everything in our country at the time of the novel's setting. The narrative germinates from the soil during one of the most heartbreaking times in our nation's history. While the author's candid and uncomfortable recounting of the insensitive language used in reference to minorities is very difficult to read, that language is also consistently measured with a clear message of the ignorance, hypocrisy, and ugliness of the characters who employ those words.

In a very real sense, the lasting offensiveness of some of the language in *To Kill a Mockingbird* has added to the poignancy of its homily on the evils of racial prejudice. We are so shocked by reading those words that it forces us to look into the mirror and remember from whence we have come—and it prompts us to search our hearts and wonder how far we still have yet to go. The novel's pure honesty about the realities of common prejudice adds its lasting relevance and urgency. It brings our past back into the light, which is crucial if we are to continue down the righteous paths of reconciliation. The American theologian Frederick

Buechner articulates the necessity of such candor: "There is a terror about light because much of what we see in the light about ourselves and our world we would rather not see, would rather not have be seen."[1] What twenty-first century readers are left with is a deep sadness and a hunger to stamp out what Atticus calls this "usual disease."

I have had the chance on several occasions to teach *To Kill a Mockingbird* in the setting of a multicultural classroom and because of the language of the novel, there are always awkward moments. I usually make a concerted effort to connect with my minority students and discuss their comfort level in dealing with the offensive language. I have found that understanding the author's brutal truthfulness concerning the viciousness of our past goes a long way toward helping my classroom through some of the uncomfortable moments caused by those references. Honesty is a sure way to highlight the enduring need for reconciliation and connectedness in our diverse society.

Tom Had to Run: Where Is Justice for the Oppressed?

Tom Robinson is accused of rape by Mayella Ewell. It is a death sentence for an African-American man in the South. The Jim Crow laws in the South of that time dictated horribly oppressive conditions for blacks, and it was not unusual for black men to be beaten or hung for even looking at a white women. Tom's accusers, the Ewell family, are considered the "trash" of Maycomb. They are despised by everyone; so it is a sad testament to the town's racism that the Ewells' word is taken over that of an innocent man.

The evidence is shallow and circumstantial. Mayella claims that she was held down, raped, and beaten by Tom. However, the facts of the case point overwhelmingly to the innocence of Tom on every count. For example, Atticus reveals, in dramatic fashion, that Bob Ewell is left-handed and that Tom's left hand is crippled from an accident. Mayella's bruises are consistent with being assaulted by someone who led exclusively with his left hand. Atticus then questions how Tom could possibly have both held her down and beaten her on the right side of her face with only one useful arm. Tom's testimony is blameless, as he honestly recounts that he was asked into Mayella's house to help her and that she unexpectedly kissed him.

The lunacy of the trial becomes even clearer when it is brought to light through Tom's testimony and Atticus's questioning of Mayella that she is consistently raped by her father. And yet justice is blinded by one simple fact: Tom is a black man and his accusers are white. No matter how much the town despises the Ewells, the jury will refuse to acquit the innocent man because of his color. As we consider the plight of Tom Robinson, we are forced to ask the question: where is justice for this man?

At the very beginning of his testimony in court, we are told that Tom has already been convicted on an assault charge. The gaping holes in the fabric of justice begin to show when Atticus leads Tom to explain why he received thirty days for disorderly conduct in his prior trouble with the law. "[Atticus] 'You were both convicted?' [Tom] 'Yes suh, I had to serve 'cause I couldn't pay the fine.'" (19). The wheels of this system we call justice seem at this point no more impartial and fair than the wheels of the cotton gin that left Tom with a crippled left arm. He has already experienced the lack of equity in the justice of society: his race determines he earns lower wages, thus he can't pay the fine in a prior conviction. This system of power that the folks of Maycomb call justice must already set Tom and the entire African-American community on edge.

As the trial progresses, Atticus questions Tom about Mayella Ewell. Tom explains his predicament to Atticus, and affirms how he carefully resisted Mayella's advances. "Mr. Finch, I tried to [resist her] 'thout bein' ugly to her . . . I didn't wanta push her or nothin'" (19). Scout goes on to explain the treatment the law's justice has leveled on Tom: "I did not understand the subtlety of Tom's predicament: he would not have dared strike a white woman under any circumstances and expect to live long, so he took the first opportunity to run—a sure sign of guilt" (19). Justice has constructed the very walls that are falling in on Tom Robinson. Was Tom innocent in his first encounter with the law? Maybe, but he served the jail sentence, not out of guilt, but because he couldn't afford to pay the fine. This system of justice is the reason that Tom knows his only option is to run from Mayella's home. If he'd stayed, her father might well have killed him, but since he runs away, he looks guilty in the eyes of society. He is in a no-win situation. Atticus articulates this dilemma for the minorities of Maycomb in his closing arguments, when he talks about the "code" as it relates to racial prejudice. The justice of the world holds no hope for Tom, and Tom knows it.

I wonder if our calls for justice sometimes are misdirected. Justice, after all, is built on the shoulders of our social codes and traditions, it is shaped with the mortar of our own self-righteous blindness, it is held up many times as a wall to separate us from the Other that we do not know and do not care to know. Is it any wonder that Tom feels trapped? Is there really fairness in our sense of justice when it lacks a connection to those who are different than we are? Justice is a rather hip term in evangelical culture today. Social justice, economic justice, even environmental justice—all are thrown around in coffee houses, university classes, and Bible studies. But I wonder sometimes if we are mistakenly latching onto language that misses the mark. Is our idea of justice an equation that lacks the power and imagination of the divine? We often define it as the proper ordering of society, but when society is overrun by the profound sin and illness of disconnection from one another, then justice is reduced to simply another form of oppression.

Growing Up to Be a Clown:
Only Children See the Inequity of Our Justice

As the prosecuting attorney completes his cross-examination of Tom Robinson, Scout's friend Dill must leave the courtroom. The way Tom is treated makes him physically sick. They run from the steps of the courthouse to the "fattest live oak tree" they can find, where Dill explains how watching Mr. Dilmer question Tom Robinson made him feel horrible: "The way that man called him 'boy' all the time an' sneered at him . . . it just makes me sick" (19). There is no one more willing to tell the truth about our relationships than children. While children certainly recognize the differences of color, language and religion, they don't seem to let it get in the way of playing together. Dill is not old enough to have been programmed into prejudice.

The children are overheard by Mr. Dolphus Raymond, a fascinating character who comes over to talk with Scout and Dill as they sit under the tree. He is a white man who is married to and has children with a black woman. This is a sinful existence in the eyes of the white townspeople—something they cannot explain or understand because they remain so disconnected from their black neighbors. Urban legend has it that Mr. Raymond is a drunk, but when he offers Dill a sip of his drink, Dill breaks out into laughter about it. The children quickly learn that he is actually not much of a drinker but carries a bottle of Coke in his bag. He explains to the children that he pretends to be a drunk when he comes into town so that the townspeople will have an explanation for his choices. He explains to Scout, "they could never, never understand that I live like I do because that is the way I want to live" (20). It is a sad commentary that the people of Maycomb can more easily believe that he is an alcoholic than think that he actually loves a woman of another race. Mr. Raymond talks to the children about prejudice and about Dill's feelings from the trial: "Things haven't caught up with that one's instinct yet. Let him get a little older and he won't get sick and cry . . . about the hell white people give colored folks, without even stopping to think that they are people, too" (20).

I think he is right. There is something special about children; they express an emotional reaction to the wrongs of the world. Having worked several different corporate jobs before I ever stepped foot in a classroom, I was amazed, my first year of teaching, by the inexorable and innate sense of fairness that children implicitly understand. I have watched many teachers lose the trust of their children because of their inability to be impartial. Maybe as we get older we just learn to accept this lack of fairness in the world and move on.

Mr. Raymond's wisdom should be a reminder to us that perhaps we *should* cry over the injustices of justice; we should come to tears when we consider the grief of the Others in our world. Somewhere along the way we become desensitized, maybe we lose hope in our power to help, or maybe we lose faith in our power to change it. There is something deeper to the sorrow of his words than the simple loss of emotion for the oppressed—I think he is talking about another childlike quality . . . *idealism.* I think idealism is exactly what Jesus is preaching to His followers when he says, "I tell you the truth, unless you change and become like little children, you will never enter the kingdom of Heaven" (Matt. 18:3, NIV). Jesus was an idealist. He called us to change the world—not to accept the hopelessness of worldly justice. I believe it is not that children necessarily see or feel the world any more honestly than we do—it is that they still have hope that it can be fixed: they cry over its inequities, they hold on to idealism because they don't know any better. Ultimately that is the quality of life to which Jesus calls us. The biblical narrative is not the story of how we will someday be swept off the earth to a sweet by and by. It is the story of people learning to believe that they must cry over sin, that they must have the courage to be idealists, that it is their work to help bring healing to the world. The lights of those who believe in hope and who practice idealism are so bright that we can't help but notice them among a world of people that have simply accepted fate and tolerated its justice. We get a glimpse into this conversion from idealism to apathy when Scout explains to us how upset and confused Dill is by the outcome of the Tom Robinson trial. Dill tells them he wants to be a clown when he grows up: "There ain't one thing in the world I can do about folks except laugh, so I'm going to join the circus and laugh my head off" (22). There is desperation in this child's wish to join the circus. When the hope for righteousness is given up, when we no longer cry about injustice, when idealism is left for practicality, we essentially join the circus of complicity with an unjust world.

No Better Than the Jury: Where Justice Falls Short

In Atticus's closing arguments, he points out the implicit weakness of this idea of justice that we all celebrate as the goal. "A court is only as sound as its jury, and a jury is only as sound as the men who make it up. I am confident that you gentlemen will review without passion the evidence you have heard . . . and restore this defendant to his family" (20). The culmination of Atticus's long and famous speech in the closing arguments of the trial comes down to the simple truth about justice: it is in the hands of the common people. It is a small component in a much larger scheme of ordering our relationships. Tom Robinson, because he is a black man, has no hope of acquittal. And for many who sit in the courtroom to observe, justice will be served. The power of these lines in the novel come to us through our understanding that each and every one of us are ultimately responsible for equity and fairness. Justice falls short when the people—you and I—are too shortsighted and disconnected from each other to recognize what it looks like. Remember, many of the Maycomb folks on this jury believe that they are good, churchgoing Christian people. Atticus's admonition that the system of justice is only as fair as the people who carry it out reminds us that justice cannot be our goal because it is not the place where true equity begins. Justice is only another system—much like religion. Both as practices, by themselves, are meaningless exercises—like the tin man with no heart—the lion with no courage—the scarecrow with no brain. You see, just as religion is empty without confession and surrender, justice can only begin with compassion. Psalm 116:5 (NIV) tells us "The LORD is gracious and righteous; our God is full of compassion." Somehow, I think that God's ideal of justice is much different from what we see in *To Kill a Mockingbird*—and in our world. It is a part of what the Christian and Jewish tradition calls righteousness.

The Defendant Is Not Guilty:
True Justice Only Grows Out of Compassion

Amidst the searing evening heat, Atticus delivers a truth to the jury that resonates in the souls of every person of the tiny Southern courtroom: he explains that there is not one reliable bit of medical evidence to prove the crime Tom is accused of ever actually happened. He continues, "It [the court] has relied instead upon the testimony of two witnesses whose evidence has not only been called into serious question on cross-examination, but has been flatly contradicted by the defendant. The defendant is not guilty, but someone in the courtroom is" (20). Atticus goes on to indict the entire courtroom when he explains that the reprehensible accusers of Tom are banking on what he describes as a "time-honored code" to convict the witness and put the evidence (Tom) of their offense away from them. The irony in this speech is that everyone in the courtroom is guilty. Justice fails because it is in the hands of these people who cannot be counted on to deliver justice because they do not practice or understand compassion.

Scout describes the scene as the jury returns to face the innocent family man: "A jury never looks at a defendant it has convicted, and when this jury came in, not one of them looked at Tom Robinson . . . Judge Taylor was polling the jury: 'Guilty . . . guilty . . . guilty . . . guilty'" (21). The verdict is an indictment of the oppression; the call "guilty" resonates around the courtroom and should settle in to the hearts of all who still read it today. There is no justice in this scene. Scout points out that her father had employed everything within the power available to free men to prove Tom's innocence, but she affirms, "in the secret courts of men's hearts Atticus had no case" (25). If justice is to be achieved, our hearts must be changed.

Perhaps when we cry for justice, we should remember the story of the Exodus. God does not simply decide to deliver the Hebrew slaves from the hands of their oppressors. He first hears their cries. Compassion is always at the heart of God's action. "I've heard their cries for deliverance from their slave masters; I know all about their pain. And now I have come down to help them" (Exodus 3:7–8, MSG). God's response to come down and deliver justice for the Hebrew slaves begins with His compassion for them. It has to be through compassion that we can connect with the suffering of others long enough to understand what justice really means. No one on the jury is truly compassionate for Tom Robinson. True compassion, as Atticus can tell you, is dangerous. When we connect with the suffering and oppressed, there is a good chance that we will also suffer their burdens—as Atticus does when he takes Tom's case. The very system of justice demonstrated in the courtroom of Maycomb is devoid of the one divine attribute that leads to justice. God's justice glimmers and flashes like stars on the dark canvas of the world—it is the promise of righteousness and order that God wishes to restore. Only when we begin to practice compassion, to connect with those we believe to be the Others, can we change the oppressive systems of justice and religion that send Tom Robinson to conviction.

The church is complicit in this conviction. The novel makes it very clear throughout that the members of the jury, those seated in the courtroom, those who silently take part in the eventual death of this innocent man, call themselves Christians. There is a beautiful text called *Freedom's Children* that I use occasionally in my classroom. I love it because it is a collection of interviews with normal everyday African-American folks who share their perspectives and experiences of living through the civil rights movements of the 1950s and 1960s. One particular interview always breaks my heart; the writer recounts the extreme prejudice she faced as a child and her confusion when she saw her white oppressors coming and going from church services. "How could they go to church on Sunday and have these kind of feelings? We'd pass their churches. They would be full of cars everywhere. When I'd see them I'd say, 'What are they even talking about in there?' It looked like they were always out in droves at church. And yet they weren't any nicer to their fellow man."[2] Makes you kind of cringe, doesn't it? Anyone who worships God should be very careful to recognize that He has a strong history of siding with the oppressed.

But compassion, the road to justice, begins with relationship—and relationships can be messy. Compassion only begins when we are able to recognize every human being, no matter what shape, size, color, or nationality, as a reflection of our creator. Prejudice goes far beyond the issue of color. As Scout reminds her brother, "Naw, Jem, I think there is just one kind of folks. Folks" (23). Jesus was the ultimate fulfillment of compassion, moving among the social outcasts and touching the untouchables. When I read about "Whites Only" signs, or African-American people having to step off of the sidewalk in order to let a white person pass, when I hear stories of black men beaten for making eye contact with white women, I think of James Roberson recounting his travels to the South as a young child: "When my dad could not get transferred, we came back [to the South]. On the way back the train stopped in a little town in northern Alabama called Decatur. I wanted something to eat, so I got off. I wasn't thinking about being black. I went in the front door of the train station. Suddenly everything stopped. A lady said, 'Get out of here, n——! You get out of here!' I was shocked. I ran out and got back on the train. I told my mom what had happened."[3] In the Jewish society of Jesus' day, social, economic, and religious prejudice was a fact of life. For example, there were very strict rules for anyone deemed to have leprosy—and any person with an unexplained skin condition might be classified as a leper. These people were forced to live in their own colonies outside of the town walls, and when they did enter the town, the law required them to yell out the warning "unclean" as they walked along. But here's how Jesus handled it: "A man with leprosy came to him and begged him on his knees, 'If you are willing, you can make me clean.' Filled with compassion, Jesus reached out his hand and touched the man. 'I am willing,' he said. 'Be clean!'"(Mark 1:40–41, NIV). Jesus was moved with compassion and touched the leper. Compassion is the touch; it is the connection to others. And that is what is lacking in the great divide of Maycomb: very few of the whites are willing to connect with their black brothers and sisters.

I have been blessed with a variety of friends, in all different shapes, colors, sizes, political persuasions, and religions. I am lucky that life has taken me to places that have allowed me to make those types of connections. It is always beautiful to have them come together in one place and connect with one another in our commonality. Diversity is a reflection of the nature of God, and it is beautiful. The early church was radical in its approach to race, gender, and class. Women, slaves, Samaritans, all took part in church leadership. Paul makes it clear that there is equality in Christ when he says, "There is neither Jew nor Greek, slave nor free, male nor female, for you are all one in Christ Jesus" (Gal. 3:28, NIV). It is this sense of equality that is absent from the Maycomb County Court.

The black members of the court scene are relegated to the balcony of the courtroom. The only whites present in the balcony are Atticus's children (Jem and Scout) and their friend, Dill. I cannot read about the segregated seating in the courtroom without thinking about the segregation of worship in Maycomb, a fact that is brought to light when Jem and Scout attend the service at Calpurnia's church. When we discuss our continued work to reconcile the color issue in our society, we should be careful to recognize the continuing fact that Sunday is still the most segregated day in America. We need to be fully cognizant as Christians that compassion can only happen with connection.

Truths That Apply to Every Race of Men: Working for God's Righteousness

In one of Atticus's brilliant moments during the closing argument, he points out the guilt of everyone in the courtroom. As he discusses the prosecution's argument, he brings to light the "code" that is responsible for convicting Tom—he summarizes it as the idea that all black men are immoral. Atticus cuts through the race issue when he implicates everyone present: "But this is a truth that applies to the human race and to no particular race of men. There is not a person in this courtroom who has never told a lie, who has never done an immoral thing . . . no man living who has never looked upon a woman without desire" (20). If Paul was present in this courtroom he might have phrased it, "We have all fallen short of the glory of God." And yet the power of Atticus's implication still resonates. The absence of true compassion that is convicting this innocent man is a result of sin.

We can look around today and see the results of a fallen world—continued prejudice. It is certainly not as pronounced as it was in the 1930s, but it is present. In many ways, minorities in our society are paying for the sins of prejudice in the twentieth century. In a 2003 US Justice Department report, about 10.4 percent of the entire African-American male population in the United States between the ages 25 to 29 was incarcerated, by far the largest racial or ethnic group. By comparison, 2.4 percent of Hispanic men and 1.2 percent of white men in that same age group were incarcerated. At the time of this report there were more African-

American men in prison than in college. In another recent report, close to 25 percent of minorities in the United States live below the federal poverty line.

Can we really look at the injustice done to Tom Robinson and pretend that there is not work left to do? As people of faith, I believe, we are to continue working for righteousness. The Hebrew word for righteousness—*tzedek*—is also understood as the chief characteristic of the Almighty. The New Testament Greek understanding of the word—*dikaios*—has a similar meaning: equitable, holy, and just. Both imply an order for the world that is perfect. Jesus begins his Sermon on the Mount with talk of righteousness. In Matthew 5:6, he says, "Blessed are those who hunger and thirst for righteousness, for they will be filled" (NIV). He is speaking to a group of oppressed people who know all too well the feeling of not having food to eat or water to drink, and He is promising them a different world.

I am fascinated when He talks about hunger and thirst. He is talking about an implicit longing for things to be right. I can only contextualize the feelings that His listeners may have had through my own experience. I have never been truly hungry, and have never truly been thirsty, but when I think of this longing, I remember the desperation I felt at hearing my forty-nine-year-old dad had died suddenly. I remember our distressed prayers for the healing of my mother-in-law as we watched her condition slowly deteriorate in the hospital. I recall the frantic prayers when we heard that my pregnant sister had stopped breathing. I think of my brother and brother-in-law fighting frantically to give my sister CPR, hoping for some signs of life. It is this type of longing and desperation that I think Jesus is calling us toward in our quest for what is right. We should feel that desperation in our efforts to bring God's righteousness to the world. Jesus was not standing before this crowd of hopeless people telling them that someday, thousands of years from now, God would take them somewhere far away where they could experience His peace and order. He was calling them to long for it as a necessity and to work to make it a reality. Righteousness is God's world order, and it begins in the hearts of people. It begins with compassion and it is the work of people of faith to make that righteousness a reality in the lives of our neighbors. It is our work as the hands, the feet, the colors of God, to bring restoration and order to creation—to all of God's people. When we lack the compassion to do that, the world becomes a hopeless place.

Scout recounts that hopelessness in the closing lines of the court scene. Earlier in the novel, she witnesses her father Atticus, an expert marksman, kill a rabid dog that is threatening their neighborhood. Curiously, this is the imagery that comes to the young girl's mind as she watches her desperate father and she realizes, as the jury returns, it will levy a horrible injustice in their verdict on Tom Robinson. "It was like watching Atticus walk into the street, raise a rifle to his shoulder and pull the trigger . . . all the time knowing that the gun was empty" (21). To me, these lines represent the measure of impotency the gospel message carries when we do not work to extend God's righteousness into the realities of the world.

While the idea of justice is continually used in so many

contexts that it begins to lose its meaning, I believe we should be cognizant of its genesis. Atticus certainly is as he closes his arguments to the jury. His final words to the jury, as recounted by Scout and Jem, are, "In the name of God, do your duty . . . In the name of God believe him" (20). We must remember that justice begins with compassion, and that compassion is the beginning of the order God intends for our world.

Such a Good Chance: No Compassion Means No Hope

The sad end to the story of Tom Robinson comes after the conviction. Tom is serving time in jail awaiting the death penalty. Atticus believes that they have a chance to appeal the conviction and have it overturned. But Tom has other ideas about justice. He tries to escape prison and is shot seventeen times by the prison guards. Atticus recounts the tragedy and Tom's loss of hope: "I guess Tom was tired of white men's chances and preferred to take his own" (24). Why would Tom ever be hopeful about his chances? He is captured in a world without compassion, without connectedness, because of his color. I think the absence of compassion always leads to a sense of hopelessness—and hopelessness on all sides. Certainly those like Mr. Link Deas, who is thrown out of the courtroom for standing up to defend Tom's good name, lost some hope, and the children struggle with hopelessness.

Tom Robinson should make us remember that the work of compassion is never done. Finding the compassion to overcome racial prejudice is specifically why Atticus explains to Scout that she should learn to climb into someone else's skin and walk around in it. It is the beginning of bridging the gaps of understanding between different people and should be our continual work. It is why the church should throw open its doors and be reaching out, instead of barricading ourselves inside. The trial is a warning to us that without compassion there can be no justice in the hearts of men—and the hearts of men control our worldly ideas of justice. Atticus tells Jem that he does not understand how the jury found it in themselves to convict an innocent man simply because of his color, yet "they've done it before and they did it tonight and they'll do it again and when they do—it seems that only children weep" (22). It is for compassion that we should remember Tom Robinson, and with the longing for compassion that we should read Tom Robinson's story. And as we read it, we should take time to remember the real tragedies: the murder of Emmett Till, the atrocity of Birmingham's Sixteenth Street Baptist Church, and the violence that the Freedom Riders faced in 1961. With desperation for compassion we should remember Rosa Parks, and the nine students who were ushered into Little Rock Central High School by the 101st Airborne. We should always be careful to remember, so that our children will not forget.

I believe that racial reconciliation will always require the constant work of compassion, but I also believe that we can make it better. I believe in the beauty of diversity—that all of God's children come together to make a beautiful reflection of His colorful image. I genuinely trust that as we work toward the common goals of compassion and connection—the keys to the kingdom of God—we can learn to appreciate each other for our differences. I think that we should always be cognizant of the work we have yet to accomplish when we read Jem Finch's words, "If there's just one kind of folks, why can't they get along with each other? If they're all alike, why do they go out of their way to despise each other?" (23).

The Parable of Raising
Jem and Scout Finch:
Parenting for Compassion

To bring up a child in the way he should go,
travel that way yourself once in a while.

—JOSH BILLINGS (1818–1885), AMERICAN AUTHOR AND HUMORIST

It's not only children who grow. Parents do too. As
much as we watch to see what our children do with their
lives, they are watching us to see what we do with ours.

—JOYCE MAYNARD (B. 1953), AMERICAN AUTHOR

ell into the novel, Scout recounts the state of father-hood as it relates to Atticus in hilarious terms. She begins, "Atticus was feeble. He was nearly fifty. When Jem and I asked him why he was so old, he said he got started late, which we felt reflected upon his abilities and manliness" (10). Scout goes on to bemoan the fact that her father really does nothing impressive, unlike the dads of her schoolmates. She points out the reality that her brother Jem is football crazy, and that while Atticus will play catch, he always cites his age when threatened with being tackled by his son. According to Scout, her father does nothing that could possibly be seen as impressive anyone (especially her classmates at school). She continues with a laundry list of grievances, pointing out us that he does not: fish, play poker, drink or smoke, drive a dump truck, carry a badge, work on a farm, or go hunting. But she seems especially troubled that, "He was nearly blind in his left eye, and said left eyes were the tribal curse of Finches" (10). The summary of her criticism is noteworthy: she tells us that all her father *really* does in sit in the house and read. Atticus is guilty of a rather unremarkable lifestyle in the eyes of his little girl; his boring and consistent lifestyle offers her nothing to brag about. Yet Atticus stands out as one of the strongest and most positive father figures in all of literature.

There are so many fascinating aspects of Scout and Jem's relationship with their father. I have always been enamored with the simple fact that they called him by his first name; throughout the story the children address him as Atticus. It represents a culture of parenthood that seems very unfamiliar to me. The way the children address him is bothersome in the initial reading of the novel, but it causes the reader to look closer at Atticus—the way his children see him. I believe it is meant to help point out his consistency as a person—he is the same man at home as he is in the community.

I certainly can't identify with Scout's list of complaints about her boring father. Like Jem, I grew up a sports fanatic. My dad was my hero, and although I don't remember him playing tackle football with us, he was always very physical in his affection. My dad was a competent athlete and as my love for basketball grew we had some epic one-on-one battles in the driveway. I was fifteen the first time I won a game, and if my memory serves me correctly, he quickly changed the nature of our competitions—from that point on we would simply play horse. I am not sure that he would ever have been pleased to hear me brag that I beat *my father* in basketball. But he died at a relatively young age, and as I near that particular age in my own life, I am always surprised at how young and inept I feel to be parenting four of my own. Most of my friends would say the same.

In my most readings of the novel, it has struck me as profound that the complaints Scout levels against her father—her wishes for him to be slightly more impressive—are outweighed by the patience and maturity of his age. Atticus seems unaffected by his children's opinion of him—he levels his parenting decisions with the same evenhandedness and life-giving communication that he uses in every other area of his life. His patience with them seems to have no limits. For example, when Scout goes through a phase of constantly cursing, Atticus explains to his brother, Jack, that all children go through a stage of using bad language, but "it dies with time when they learn they're not attracting attention with it" (9). Of the many attributes Atticus demonstrates in the way he parents, it is his consistency of character that separates him the most. He is not a man whose aim is to simply please his children, just as he is not interested in conforming to the usual views of the town. He is guided by a deep sense of character. It is difficult for many of us in today's culture to say no to our kids; we seem intent on not disappointing them, on remaining popular with them. It is often true that we do this to make up for time we do not spend with them. We fear we will lose them if they are angry with us, and yet nothing could be farther from the truth.

Unlike those of us who do most of our parenting in our twenties, thirties, and forties, Atticus carries the wisdom of years into his dealings with the children. In his time with them, his expressions of love, his discipline and teaching, and the way he entrusts the immediate community to invest in the maturing of his children, we find a sagelike approach that comes from life experience. He parents with wisdom and an implicit sense of trust that I think we could all learn from.

He Sat in the Living Room and Read: Time Well Spent

If there is one thing we learn in the novel, well before Scout's complaints about her father, it is that she knew how to read at a very young age. As her older brother tells their friend Dill, "Scout yonder's been readin' ever since she was born" (1). It is one of the first personal traits that we discover about our narrator. Scout gets herself into trouble with the new first grade teacher when she demonstrates literacy well beyond her years. Miss Caroline Fisher tersely instructs Scout to inform her father that he is not qualified to teach her how to read. Scout reacts with complete indignation to her objections: "He hasn't taught me anything . . . Why, he's so tired at night he just sits in the livingroom and reads" (2). Scout, as a first grader, explains that she has never remembered not possessing the ability to read. As she struggles to remember how she came by her skill with words, she tells us, "I could not remember when the lines above Atticus's moving finger separated into words, but I had stared at them all the evenings in my memory . . . anything Atticus happened to be reading when I crawled into his lap every night" (2). It becomes apparent to us that evenings in the Finch household are spent with the entire family gathered together in the study. We are left to ascertain for ourselves that Scout can read at such a young age because she spends every evening in her father's lap as he reads. It is true that the best gift we can impart to our children is our time. For Atticus, spending evenings with his children is routine.

Work culture will never provide incentives for the time us spend with our children. I have rarely seen a company reward the man or woman who demonstrated the highest commitment to their kids. It is clear in the novel that Atticus understands where his work fits into the order of his life. His children meet him at home for lunch, they run to greet him at the end of the street after work each evening, they have dinner together, and they end their evenings reading together. Atticus is very present in their lives even during the Tom Robinson trial, when he is at his busiest; he seems to maintain a higher commitment to his children. And when he is present with Jem and Scout, he offers them his attention.

When we are physically present with our children, often we do not offer them our presence—our attention is not with them. I am guilty of being one of the most plugged-in people that I know. I love the speed of modern communication and thrive on social networking, my iPhone, my e-mail, and the constant connection that it provides to my community. One fall day several years ago I was driving to the grocery store with my youngest son, talking away on my cell phone to a friend in another town (a practice I've discontinued in light of the proven dangers). I remember sitting at a stop light when I realized this beautiful little person behind me was just chatting away, completely unaware that I was not paying attention to him. He was in the middle of telling me how much he loved me. I looked in my rearview mirror at him, smiled, and promptly hung up the phone. Since that moment, as much as possible, I try to stay away from my computer and phone on the evenings and weekends. I'm not always successful, but I have been more aware of ensuring that the focus of my time spent with my kids is actually on them. It is not enough to simply be present; they long for our attention. When we spend time with them but are distracted with work, phones, e-mails, we are demonstrating where they stand in our list of priorities. Work, connection, community: all of these things are good when placed in the proper order of our lives. We should learn to turn off our digital and electronic world, focus our attention on the people under our care. And as Atticus demonstrates for us, there is certainly no greater way to spend time with your family than gathering together around a good book.

The practices of the Finch household are so elemental to Scout's childhood that she ends the narrative in a place where she feels the safest and most valued. The last scene of the novel takes place with Atticus reading to Scout, "I willed myself to stay awake, but the rain was so soft and the room was so warm and his voice was so deep and his knee was so snug that I slept" (31). With all of the excitement and drama of the novel's final pages, Scout ends her story in the most important of places: her father's lap.

It is also essential to understand that Atticus does not parent alone. Calpurnia, who is much more than just their cook and house-keeper, plays a very strong maternal role in the lives of the children. Scout describes Calpurnia as ever present in her life, and as she matures begins to view her as a strong model of feminine influence. Although Scout is hardly old enough to recognize Calpurnia's significance to the family, it becomes very apparent how much Atticus values her role as surrogate mother to the children. He tells them that the family couldn't survive one day without her: "You think about how much Cal does for you and you mind her" (3). I've read that close to 10 percent of America's children live in a single parent household, which makes me realize how important our investment can be in the lives of other children. Atticus views the role Calpurnia plays as essential to the lives of his children.

Scout tells us early in the novel that her mother died when she was very young and admits that she never really felt the affects of her mother's absence.. but this remark is weighted with Calpurnia's presence in her life, which she describes as, "She was always ordering me out of the kitchen, asking me why I couldn't behave as well as Jem . . . and calling me home when I wasn't ready to come" (1). At the beginning of one of my favorite sequences in the novel, Scout describes the care with which Calpurnia meticulously prepares their clothes when she takes them to visit her church, the African-American church in Maycomb. It is evident that Calpurnia, values these children as her own, and, as parents often are, is intent on them making a good impression.

A Stinging Smack and Reading to Mrs. Dubose: Discipline as an Expression of Love

Walter Cunningham, Scout's classmate, comes to school with no lunch on the first day, and after a scuffle in the schoolyard at recess, Jem invites Walter over to the Finch house for lunch. During lunch, Scout is amazed as Walter discusses farm business with her father with a maturity well beyond a first grader. But when their houseguest begins to pour syrup on his lunch, Scout is highly offended. "Walter poured syrup on his vegetables and meat with a generous hand. He would probably have poured it into his milk glass had I not asked what the sam hill he was doing" (3). Calpurnia quickly rebukes Scout and sends her to the kitchen.

Behind the closed door, she scolds Scout, explaining how she is supposed to treat guests in their home: "'If you can't act fit to eat at the table you can just set here and eat in the kitchen!' Calpurnia sent me through the swinging door to the dining room with a stinging smack" (3). Calpurnia has no problem disciplining Scout for her mistreatment of Walter Cunningham.

Discipline seems to be one of the most challenging aspects of childrearing for parents. I have on many occasions listened to a parent complain that he just doesn't know how to discipline his child. I think this is a result of some confusion about discipline—discipline is not the same as punishment. Discipline is simply how we teach our children. It is a vital aspect of parenting if our children are to know right from wrong, how to respect others, and what behaviors are acceptable. Psychologists tell us that children who are disciplined are also children who feel secure, loved, self-confident, are self-disciplined, and, in turn, have lower stress levels.

Atticus's discipline of the children is always bent toward instructing them. This is borne out in the illustration of the trouble Jem gets himself into with Mrs. Henry Lafayette Dubose. After facing the sick old woman's insults day after day, Jem finally loses his cool and goes raging into her front yard, destroying her flowers with a baton he had bought for Scout. He ends his tirade by snapping the gift in half. When Atticus returns from work that evening, he questions Jem about the incident and tells him that his actions are indefensible. "'I strongly advise you to go down and have a talk with Mrs. Dubose,' said Atticus. 'Come straight home afterward'" (11). Atticus is teaching Jem that he must own up to his actions. He does not offer to go to Mrs. Dubose's house with Jem and help him apologize. One of the greatest lessons we can teach our children is that they should take responsibility for their own missteps. The prospect of Jem going alone to apologize to Mrs. Dubose is a terrifying proposition, so scary in the eyes of the children, that Scout believes Atticus might be sending Jem to his death. While it might seem that Mrs. Dubose deserves some of the blame in this matter—because of the terrible things she yells at the children each day when they pass her house—Atticus never acknowledges this. The focus of his discipline, or lesson, is to make Jem understand that he should be in control of his own actions, no matter what the situation.

I was about Jem's age when I had my first (and last) school fistfight. It happened directly in front of my locker; it was a blur with the rush of adrenaline and people quickly gathering, but I mainly remember teachers swooping in to separate me and my sparring partner. I came home that day with butterflies in my stomach and went straight to the basketball court in an effort to avoid Dad (my father was a high school principal for a time, and in many ways a formidable, stern-looking man). I remember hearing him come out of the back door and begin making his way toward me on the court. He had received a call from the school; I was devastated. Growing up in a family of educators, I knew that my punishment would be swift. I was disarmed a bit when he stepped onto the court and began to rebound for me without saying a word. At this point I was in tears, and as we shot baskets I shamefully recounted the events of the fight. I will never forget his level demeanor and the even expressions of his response. After listening, he held the ball for a moment. He said he didn't blame me for defending myself; he understood that I was ashamed of my actions, but that I would go to the principal, teachers, and student to apologize. He made it clear he was going to support whatever course of discipline the school decided to take. He passed the ball to me, patted me on the shoulder, and turned to walk back inside. I vividly remember the horror of serving what they called in-school suspension for three long days. Dad never mentioned the incident to me again. He didn't punish me; he taught me. He was determined that I take responsibility for my actions.

The teaching aspect of discipline in the case of Mrs. Dubose continues when Jem returns from apologizing. He tells Atticus she has requested that he come to her house and spend two hours reading aloud to her every day for an entire month. Atticus responds, "Then you'll do it for a month" (11). Atticus makes it clear to Jem that he will follow through with the consequences of losing his cool. The children actually survive reading to Mrs. Dubose for a month, and days later they learn that Mrs. Dubose has died from her long battle with illness. It is at this point that Atticus explains to them that he would have made them read to her anyway. He tells them there was something he wanted them to learn from Mrs. Dubose. He explains her illness to them. It is a clear and powerful lesson to the children about courage, but Atticus is also teaching them about compassion. By enforcing Mrs. Dubose's wish, Scout and Jem are able to better comprehend her circumstances when Atticus explains her addiction to morphine. As people of faith we need to consider that our goal should be to raise children, not as doctors, lawyers, politicians or professional athletes, but first and foremost to be compassionate people.

Miss Maudie, Reverend Sykes, and Miss Caroline Fisher: Trusting the Community With Our Children

Although the role of Atticus in their lives is essential, many of the greatest lessons that the children learn throughout the novel are imparted by the people of Maycomb. Atticus seems to trust the community with his children, and while their family is ordered and secured in the rhythms of eating together and spending evenings reading, he is comfortable allowing them to explore the world and learn from these people. For Scout, their neighbor Miss Maudie becomes a significant influence. Maudie is the female protagonist of the novel who shares insights about Atticus, religion, nature, and truths about the people of Maycomb. Maudie also plays an important role in guiding and protecting Scout as she comes to terms with the question of what it means to be a lady in a Southern society full of gender expectations. She seems always a part of the landscape when the children are playing outside; she bakes for them and treats them as her own. Possibly the most significant role Maudie plays in her maternal treatment of the children comes as she helps them understand their father and the nature of his character. She explains that while many people behave much differently behind closed doors than they do in public, their father is unique. "Atticus Finch is the same in his house as he is on the public streets" (5).

The children are given direction even beyond the safety of their own street, though. At a break during the Tom Robinson trial, Mr. Dolphus Raymond shares a Coke with the children and explains his lifestyle to them. It is a wonderful lesson for Scout and her friend Dill on the evils of prejudice. And he again affirms to them the strength of Atticus's character: "Miss Jean Louise, you don't know your pa's not a run-of-the-mill man, it'll take a couple years for that to sink in—you haven't seen enough of the world yet" (20). The children also connect with the pastor of the African-American community in Maycomb when they visit his church with Calpurnia. Through his sermon they learn a wonderful lesson in how the community should care for one another and, more significantly, they are exposed to the culture of their neighbors. Later, Reverend Sykes shepherds the children into the balcony and sits with them during the Tom Robinson trial. He takes responsibility for them, and even questions Jem about the appropriateness of Scout being there to hear the sordid details of the alleged rape. At one point, Scout even falls asleep and takes a short nap on his arm while at the trial the jury is deliberating. The reverend demonstrates to the children his deep reverence for their father when he asks them to stand out of respect for Atticus as he leaves the courtroom.

We certainly live in a much different world today. We are a transient society, much less connected than the residents of

Maycomb. Most parents would not allow their children to spend time sitting on a neighbor's porch. In many cases, we are not even comfortable with extended family members supervising our children. Yet consider all you learned from the adults who took an interest in you; I think you may find that you were shaped as much by other people as you were by your own parents. I remember the church people, teachers, and coaches that my parents empowered to have an impact in my life. I know now that my parents didn't always agree with these other people, but it was rarely made known to me—their authority over me was never disparaged.

The scene that best reflects Atticus's attitude involves the new teacher Miss Caroline Fisher. Poor Miss Fisher is a bit of a novice. Not only is she dealing with the realities of Maycomb's culture, she is also struggling to learn the practicalities of teaching children. She is outraged when she finds that Scout, a first grader, can already read. She sends Scout home with the explicit instruction that her father is not qualified to teach reading and that he should stop immediately. It is a hilarious scene. Miss Caroline is probably months of experience away from realizing her mistake; she is very young. Most parents today, upon hearing this, would charge down to the school to accost the first-year teacher. While Atticus clearly disagrees with Ms. Fisher, he handles the situation in a completely different manner, saying to Scout, "If you'll concede the necessity of going to school, we'll go on reading every night just as we always have . . . you'd better not say anything at school about our agreement . . . I'm afraid our activities would be received with considerable disapprobation by the more learned authorities" (3).

Atticus doesn't deride Miss Fisher's authority by pointing out her ignorance, he simply assures Scout that they can continue to read each evening. On some level Atticus is showing a trust or at least deference to Miss Fisher's commitment to educate his child.

We might be mistaken by shielding our children from our neighbors, mistaken in buying into the idea that the world is no longer safe for them. Although just turning on the evening news can be motivation enough to keep our children away from others, I think our distrust has more to do with our own isolation from community. Maybe we don't trust each other with our children simply because we do not take the time to know each other. While Atticus teaches his children to find the best in everyone, he maintains an implicit confidence in the goodness of people. The characters Jem and Scout encounter make an invaluable contribution to their upbringing, and most of them communicate a profound respect for Atticus that is borne from knowing him.

In many ways, our splintered communities, our neighborhood of strangers, are a result of our own lifestyle as parents. When we treat teachers, coaches, neighbors, and church people with a sense of distrust, I wonder if we aren't perpetuating our own sense of isolation from others in our children. My wife and I are deeply appreciative of the people at church, at school, and around the neighborhood who take the time to make an investment in our children—even when we disagree with them.

We should all feel a connection to the children in our community; what could be done if we all made an effort to help make an impact in the life of a child? Early Christians showed a sense of responsibility for children that was modeled by Jesus, and it had a major impact on the world. Before the early church movement, children were treated as less than human. In most cultures, unwanted children were thrown to the streets or worse. I have read that Christians were one of the first subcultures to begin adoption and to view children with dignity. The early church literally ushered in a completely new respect for the rights of children and an ethic of how they should be cared for that had not existed before. It is interesting to consider that their motivation for this had much to do with their story—one of being adopted by a father into a divine community.

Bad Language and Honesty: Being Real with Our Children

Another compelling aspect of Atticus's style of parenting is his complete honesty with his children. He is confronted with explaining some pretty difficult circumstances to Scout and Jem throughout the novel. The family is faced with the town's bitter reaction to his commitment to defend Tom Robinson. Atticus is forced to explain racism, death, and rape to Scout. At one point, Scout, who is momentarily fascinated with cursing, asks her Uncle Jack to explain the meaning of "whore-lady." Jack responds to her question with a story—essentially avoiding the question all together. Atticus tells his brother that he mustn't be afraid to answer the children's questions with honesty. But, he explains further, ". . . don't make a production of it. Children are children, but they can spot an evasion quicker than adults, and evasion simply muddles 'em" (9). Atticus is right; sometimes we go out of our way to protect our children from the realities of life—realities more pressing than just bad language.

I have discovered through conversations with my eleven-year-old—my oldest son—that kids can always sense when you avoid the truth. We have a responsibility to be truthful with our children about life—in measures that they can comprehend. We struggled with this concept several years ago with him. He lived through the sudden death of my sister and her child, the death of my wife's mother, and the death of his great-grandparents, all in the short span of three years. We learned, through that process, the necessity of telling the truth, even when the questions are tough (like, why does God let people die?). When we protect our children from realities, I think we make it more difficult for them to deal with life.

I have noticed that parents I work with today seem quick to shield their children from anything uncomfortable, and I do sympathize; much of the time parenting feels like trial and error. But we underestimate the resilience and understanding of our children. I realize the truth is more uncomfortable for me than it is for my children sometimes. I am learning with my oldest son that honesty, no matter how difficult, is always the best solution. While he is far more aware of the realities of death and failure, he also possesses an untimely appreciation for other people and for the beautiful moments we experience as a family. When I talk to him at bedtime, he consistently amazes me with his perspectives on the special moments of his life—especially those involving his brothers and sisters. He often comments about a picturesque instant of everyday life that is beyond the understanding of most eleven-year-olds, and, frankly, beyond what I often take time to notice as an adult.

Any educator will quickly tell you that if you don't know the answer to a question, honesty is the best way to motivate a classroom to search it out. I use this consistently (even when I do know the answers) to empower my students to find the right answers by employing the wealth of resources we are given through information technology. I have learned that honesty with my children—about myself, about the world, about their world—is not as scary for them most times as it is to me. My honesty actually empowers them to be honest—to be better human beings.

The Same Man Inside His Home: Transparency and Modeling What It Means to Be a Compassionate Human Being

I was fortunate to begin teaching not long after we had our second child. With four, now, I am so grateful for my chosen professions of writing and teaching. It does not take long in a classroom of children to understand that they notice everything you do. Your every movement, change of attire, haircut, and communication is noted with great interest. Author Robert Fulghum articulated this beautifully when he said, "Don't worry that [your children] never listen to you, worry that they are always watching you."[1]

Isn't that the greatest challenge of parenting? No matter what we tell our children, they learn by observing us. The thought certainly is sobering when I think about the times I am impatient, angry, or frustrated; our children will pattern their lives after us in many ways. They will model our faith and our relationships with others.

Atticus models the type of life he wants his children to lead not only with his words like "I do my best to love everybody" (11), but with his actions: his concern for Mrs. Dubose, his connection with the neighbors on the street, the way he treats Mayella Ewell on the witness stand, his commitment to Tom Robinson, and his connection to the town's African-American community. He teaches Jem and Scout how to live with a sense of responsibility for their neighbors. Late in the novel, Atticus's impact on Scout's coming of age is made clear when she proudly recounts the words of Miss Maudie: she tells Jem that Atticus is the same in the house as he is in public. His role as a parent is made clear when he explains to Scout why he must take the Tom Robinson case because of his principles, no matter what the town thinks. He says, "sometimes we have to make the best of things . . . when you and Jem are grown, maybe you'll look back on this with some compassion and some feeling that I didn't let you down" (11). Atticus ultimately lives his life with a deep awareness that his actions will be reflected in the nature of his children as adults. Psychiatrist Karl Menninger is famously quoted as having said that what's done to children, they will do to society—but the ethic that Atticus teaches us as people of faith holds a much higher aim than this. Sure, he demonstrates the undeniable truth that the behavior we model for our children will be replicated in their actions in our society. More importantly, though, the Finch children will practice compassion to the world. Scout indicates she is growing under her father's direction as a compassionate human being at the close of the novel, when she stands on the Radley front porch, and does exactly as her father has so eloquently taught her—she envisions what life would be like if she were to walk around in Boo Radley's shoes.

The Parable of the
Last Word: Communicating
to Build Community

The unaffected language of real feeling and
benevolence is easily understood, and is never ridiculous.

—Maria Edgeworth (1767–1849), English novelist

Oppressive language does more than represent violence;
it is violence; does more than represent the limits of
knowledge; it limits knowledge.

—Toni Morrison (b. 1931), accepting the Nobel Prize
in literature, 7 December 1993

B ob Ewell stopped Atticus Finch on the steps of the post office, spat in his face, and threatened him in the presence of many on looking town folks. Atticus explains that Bob meant what he said at the time he said it. "Jem, see if you can stand in Bob Ewell's shoes a minute. I destroyed his last shred of credibility at that trial . . . The man had to have some kind of comeback, *his kind always does*" (23, emphasis mine). While Atticus failed to rescue Tom Robinson from the clutches of a racist jury, he succeeded in allowing Bob Ewell to reveal himself as a liar to all of Maycomb. Atticus is explaining Bob's threat to Jem and Scout to alleviate their uneasiness with the confrontation. The Ewells are uneducated and isolated from the rest of Maycomb County, and Atticus is pointing out how this affects how they communicate. Of the many differences that separate Atticus from his antagonist, possibly the most noticeable is the manner in which he interacts with others.

We have been given no greater ability to heal or to harm one another than through the power of our words. Every culture has a saying about the fierce impact of the spoken word. The wisdom writers of the Old Testament remind us that "death and life are in the power of the tongue" (Prov. 18:21, NKJV). As a writer and an educator, I am deeply cognizant of the power of words. We certainly can speak death and life, hope and despair, togetherness or division into the lives of others. I can recount many stories about the power of language: one friend developed an eating disorder because of the harsh words her father delivered, and one pastor lost his ministry because of bitter rumors spread by an elder in his church. It is clear to me that our mouths are powerful tools.

It seems more difficult to escape the stories about people of faith and our irresponsibility with language simply because we should know better. I spoke with a fellow educator brought to tears by the harshness of e-mails and phone messages left by a parent—who she later discovered was the head pastor of a large church just a block from her school. I am reminded of a holiday shopping experience with my children standing at the jewelry counter, where we witnessed a verbal assault so egregious that it could have been an episode of the *Jerry Springer Show*. The volume and tone of the shopper's language insinuated the gravity of a life-and-death situation; the object of her ire was the sale price of a cross necklace.

I wonder sometimes if the frequency of the language we exchange without human contact via e-mail, texting, Twitter, or cell phones has not desensitized us. Communication is a deeply spiritual matter, but there is often no flesh and blood visible when we are exchanging words this way. More and more, we operate as if we are truly islands unto ourselves, as isolated as the Ewells. Yet we were made to live in community with each other. Whatever the reason, it seems to me that we have developed an easy violence with our language. We are becoming a culture who, like Bob Ewell, must always have "some kind of comeback." However, one of the most profound aspects of *To Kill a Mockingbird* is discovered when we notice that our heroes and heroines are not people driven to have the last word.

When Scout asks Atticus why most of the town thinks he is wrong to defend Tom Robinson, Atticus responds, "They are certainly entitled to think that, and they are entitled to full respect for their opinions, . . . but before I can live with other folks, I've got to live with myself" (11). Considering the racism displayed by the people of the town, Atticus's explanation might seem a little confusing. We all would affirm that we deeply admire the character of Atticus Finch and the way he conducts himself, although, frankly, I am not optimistic that if Atticus were a real person in today's culture he would be acknowledged as such an admirable protagonist. Turn on your television set, read different news sites, listen to politicians, open up a blog or two, spend a little time observing at virtually any place of business, or maybe even attend a church board meeting: we are becoming a society that values having the last and the loudest word. Our heroes are the people who prove to everyone, at any cost, that they are correct. It doesn't matter how raucous, how terse, or how violent the communication must be—it seems we are willing to join the fray at the expense of anyone, if it will only advance our political, religious, economic, or personal agenda.

I am quite certain that Atticus would go quite unnoticed by popular culture. He would not be the proud winner of the argument or a man known for always getting his way. He would never be the loudest voice in the room, and he would certainly never brandish the truth like a weapon to beat opposing viewpoints into submission. He would appear reserved on the periphery of our lunch tables, business counters, classrooms, and church pews. He would demonstrate communicative qualities foreign to today's culture. And I sincerely doubt he would be forcefully drawing attention to himself, or boasting of his accomplishments to gain everyone's respect. His language would probably be perceived as too respectful of the opinions of others, and too conscious of his relationship to his neighbors to attract our admiration.

I wonder if the aggressive nature of our communication, our forceful affirmations, and our need to be right more than to be connected, is quickly and not so quietly undermining our inherent need for community. We Christian folks, whose single purpose it is to spread hope in the world, seem to be some of the worst offenders. We have moved from being a people who were named "little Christs" by the popular culture of Rome, to people who are exceedingly preoccupied with labeling and promoting ourselves as followers of Christ. The Bible is full of advice and warnings about the power of language, with over twenty references to communicating with one another in the Proverbs alone. The fascinating aspect of the characters in the Mockingbird narrative (Atticus in particular) is that they model this same type of biblical wisdom. Colossians encourages us to "Let your conversation be always full of grace" (4:6, NIV). James spends an extravagant amount of time in his letter addressing the power of communication, "My dear brothers, take note of this: Everyone should be quick to listen, slow to speak and slow to become angry" (1:19, NIV). The characters of *To Kill a Mockingbird* model a much different ethic when it comes to communication and truth telling than what is practiced in our culture today. It is necessary for people of faith to model responsible communication in our daily lives if we are to fulfill our obligation to be reflections of the nature of God. Our call is to speak words not born of our own desires and agendas, but words that give life and encourage community with our neighbors. We should approach each communication with an awareness of the divine nature of our interaction. There is a steady undercurrent of grace in the way that Atticus and some of the other characters speak in the novel, which is something we can certainly learn from.

Are We All Deaf Witnesses?
Listening Is an Essential Part of Communication

Scout tells us much about the way Atticus communicates with people throughout the novel. During the Tom Robinson trial she says that, "I had never heard Atticus raise his voice in my life, except to a deaf witness" (17). Volume is not the quality of communication that connects us with others. I used to speculate that the pure noise of our constant connection to media was raising the volume of our dialogue; we are becoming like Atticus's deaf witness. But I think that it goes a little deeper than that. We are not nearly as interested in *listening* as we are in being *heard*. I know from growing up in a family of talkers that the absence of listeners can generate a good bit of noise around the dinner table—but we have all, in our maturity, realized that we have to try to hear each other. It is Atticus's quality of listening to others that allows him to refrain from raising his voice.

Everyone has witnessed a disagreement that moves quickly from dialogue to shouting. Culture encourages us to be aggressive and assertive, but in practice these qualities lead to communication that is devoid of listening, which is the key to exchange. The pure volume of communication is actually a form of violence. Violence occurs in the absence of compassion and in our unwillingness to hear. We are left with only our selfish motivation to be heard, to leave our mark on the Other with the pure strength of our voice.

I worked several public relations jobs when I first graduated from college. It is a profession that supposedly employs, or at least implies, a mastery over language. But I never really comprehended the authority of words until I began my career as an educator; then I began to understand the not-so-subtle nuances of communication. Communication, the beginnings of compassion, is a connection; a true exchange. The Bible goes so far as to say that those who do not listen are fools. Proverbs tell us that "Fools are headstrong and do what they like; wise people take advice"" (12:15, MSG). I am still discovering that while often the most celebrated educators are great orators, the most effective teachers are first and foremost exceptional listeners. I believe that not only are we to lower the volume and violence of our language, we must also close our mouths and learn to listen before we speak.

Speaking Sharply: Softening the Tones
of Our Communication

Scout establishes Atticus's tone as a communicator when she tells us about a conversation with her Aunt Alexandra: "But the only time I ever heard Atticus speak sharply to anyone was when I once heard him say, 'Sister, I do the best I can with them!'" (81). Considering all that Atticus confronts in defending Tom Robinson, standing down a lynch mob, dealing with the angry Mrs. Dubose, and having Bob Ewell spit in his face, this observation by Scout is dramatic. Atticus is constantly faced with situations that almost demand that he speak sharply, and yet he never does. When I was in college, we used to sit back and laugh at the late-night talk circus shows, with people on stage screaming at one another and fighting. I am sure you remember them. Every episode included a person or two who felt there was a score to settle—that they had been wronged in some way. Despite the host's cute resolutions at the close of each episode, the sad truth is that the theme of those shows always centered on some type of relational disconnectedness. When we feel we are being slighted in some way, we must fight off the urge to use the same type of communicative violence.

It is as if we take pride in our aggressiveness, and it is born out in the tones of our language. We vote for the politician who wins the argument and feel smug when someone who espouses our worldview puts an opponent in his place. Atticus, who is shown to be a brilliant speaker during the trial of Tom Robinson, swears off the sharpness of communication, even when faced with matters of life and death. As a teacher, I learned quickly that one terse line can empty out a good measure of relational trust and that my tone can be essential in building connections with these children whom I value so much. Atticus, however, is aware of the deeper ordering of the universe in his dealings with people. There is a beautiful restraint to the tone of his words. The protagonists of Maycomb demonstrate for us a deep value in connecting with others—even if they do not win the argument.

Calling Her "Ma'am": The Bravery of Respect in the Face of Belligerence

One of the clearest and most deliberate examples of how we should communicate with people takes place in how Atticus handles the miserable Mrs. Dubose. An old woman who yells at Scout when she passes by—"Don't you say hey to me, you ugly girl!" (11)—Mrs. Dubose is guilty of terrible name-calling. She accosts the children with insults that would infuriate any parent. Scout tells us, "When we came to her house, Atticus would sweep off his hat . . . and say, 'Good evening, Mrs. Dubose! You look like a picture this evening.' . . . He would tell her the courthouse news, and would say that he hoped with all his heart she'd have a good day tomorrow . . . It was times like these when I thought my father, who hated guns and had never been to any wars, was the bravest man who ever lived" (11). Honestly, when I imagine my own children being treated this way by a neighbor, saying good evening would probably not even be close to my initial response. But Atticus is aware that Mrs. Dubose is a dying woman; he is conscious of her humanness, and ultimately her need for others. His response appears noble to us, but for him is just a way of life, part of an ethic he models for the children as they begin to face the insults of the town because of their father's defense of Tom Robinson. The true test of who we are comes out when we are faced with these types of situations. Atticus is divinely aware of the humanity of those same Maycomb folks, and refuses to respond to them with the violence of language.

His approach to communication is quickly noted by Mayella Ewell. She is enraged on the witness stand by Atticus's politeness. Although she is abused, fragile, and in some ways a sympathetic figure, Mayella is also an antagonist in the novel. Her testimony in court is a web of lies and deceit that will send an innocent man to his death. Atticus makes it clear to the children that his sympathy for Mayella does not stretch so far as to allow her to lie about Tom Robinson, yet he is still respectful of her humanity while he questions her. In fact, it is made clear to us that Atticus may be the only character in the novel who has ever shown Mayella this type of respect. As he questions her, he politely refers to her as "ma'am." Being accustomed to the violence of her father's language and assuming Atticus is ridiculing her, Mayella lashes out at him. The judge presiding over the case must stop the court proceeding to explain to her that it is simply Atticus's nature to communicate respectfully to people. "We've done business in court for years and years, and Mr. Finch is always courteous to everybody. He's not trying to mock you, he's trying to be polite" (18). Judge Taylor makes it clear that Atticus's language is only a reflection of his character.

I wonder if it would help us to remember that God's grace has been extended to us when we are facing difficult situations where no grace is being offered by another human being. Nothing defines our faith, the current condition of our soul, who we truly are, like the words we use when we are attacked or under duress. Jesus references this when He says, "The good man brings good things out of the good stored up in his heart . . . out of the overflow of his heart his mouth speaks" (Luke 6:45, NIV). The results of our responses, good or bad, are not always celebrated by others, but they are always noticed. We should be conscious of the eternal ramifications of our communication. For Atticus, there is no reward in being kind to a dying lady or being polite to a dishonest witness. Both seem fruitless in their result. Yet I am left wondering if the entire community of Maycomb is fascinated with the spirit of this man's gentleness.

Mr. Link Deas Interrupts the Court: Having the Courage to Tell the Truth

Swearing off the violence of communication and learning how to listen does not mean that we must remain silent about the truth. During the trial of Tom Robinson, Tom's former employer, Link Deas, reaches a point where he cannot control himself. He rises from his seat as the prosecutor is approaching Tom on the witness stand and announces to the court, "That boy's worked for me eight years an' I ain't had a speck o'trouble outa him. Not a speck" (19). Deas is one of the few in the courtroom outraged by the atrocity of what is happening, and he is moved to speak the truth. I have always noticed the absence of exclamation marks in his declaration. Link Deas doesn't yell. He is promptly reprimanded by Judge Taylor and removed from the premises. His interjection is necessary because he is speaking truth into a situation that is full of pretense. Perhaps he does not yell in desperation because he is certain of the truth of what he is speaking. In fact, the truth is evident to all who are present in the courtroom.

The communication of the truth presents a challenge for people of faith. We have a responsibility to tell the truth in all of our communication. Reading the courtroom scene, one gets the sense that Mr. Deas cannot control himself any longer—he is sure of it and is moved to affirm it. Mr. Deas allows us to define the nature of how we must deliver truth in our world. He is not speaking out for his own well-being—his truth telling has the Other in mind.

Telling the truth is not always simple; it is not always black and white. Much of what we inject ourselves into is not truth telling, but perspective telling. It is the difference between the authenticity of sharing the truth, and the crusade of wielding our own perspective. I can't tell you how many times I have jumped into a conversation when I felt that someone was misdirected in his spiritual or political direction. One hundred percent of the time my argument (my perspective telling) has absolutely no impact on him. When we offer truth outside the context of that understanding, outside of the circumstance of being moved with compassion, away from the framework of relationship, our words can become nothing more than propaganda.

The truth must be identified when it matters, but it is always there and present, whether we call attention to it or not—it is written on the hearts of men (see 2 Cor. 3:2). I question if one of the greatest disservices we contribute to culture is not found in our incessant charging around in defense of the truth. For some reason we seem so threatened by science, technology, politics—whatever is opposing our worldview—that we feel it is our job to loudly patrol our communities armed with arguments about the "truth." Just as Link Deas is confident that the truth is present in the hearts of every man in the courtroom, we should also be confident in every situation that the truth is written on the hearts of men. I am not sure that God ever meant to hire us on as a public relations staff; I think He intended us rather to be models of His compassion—receptacles of His grace—living representatives of a truth written so deeply into creation that it needs no propaganda. We must remember that truth is a movement of compassion and that it is the first step toward freedom.

He Looked Like His Stomach Hurt:
The Sadness of Telling the Truth

Sometimes there may be a sadness that comes with our obligation to tell the truth. Atticus is questioning Mayella Ewell, the lonely young woman with no friends, sexually abused by her own father, while she is attempting to send an innocent man to his death. Atticus begins to press Mayella with a series of questions and exposes her as a liar to the entire court; as he finishes, Scout tells us that she notices a sadness in his demeanor when he turns away from the witness, "but Mayella's face was a mixture of terror and fury" (18). Several lines later Scout explains, "Somehow, Atticus had hit her hard in a way that was not clear to me, but it gave him no pleasure to do so" (18). It seems everywhere we look in our culture we find people who receive much gratification out of being right—setting the Other straight. Atticus understands the weight of truth telling. A compassionate sharing of the truth should be taxing on us. There is no satisfaction shown by Atticus in this scene, no triumphant smile, no sense that he feels victorious. We should be careful with the importance of the truth and never communicate it with pretense. This may be particularly difficult at times; it is in our nature as human beings to want to be confirmed right. It is not the truth that pains Atticus here; the truth is a necessity. Atticus comprehends how powerfully the truth is going to hit this pathetic young woman, and he feels the weight of it. He seems to understand the consequence of wielding the truth and takes no satisfaction in seeing its power to humiliate those who ignore its eternal sway.

The Maycomb Missionary Tea and Racism:
The Dangers of Political and Religious Correctness

When Atticus comes face to face with the political, religious, and social demon of racism, he does not mince his words. In a conversation with his brother Jack he calls it "Maycomb's usual disease" and when he is forced to confront it at the trial of the innocent black man accused of rape and assault, he calmly and evenly delivers the truth of the accusers' guilt to the jury: "What was the evidence of her offense? Tom Robinson, a human being . . . She did something that in our society is unspeakable: she kissed a black man . . . No code mattered to her before she broke it, but it came crashing down on her afterwards" (20). Atticus is speaking directly to the jury, the court, the town, and illuminating the truth they all know in their hearts. Tom's innocence is clear, and yet the only thing that will convict him is this time-honored code of racism.

Something occurred to me recently as I read these lines, something horrible and unconscionable but true. In the time and setting of the novel, the Deep South of the 1930s and beyond, it was deemed politically correct to practice this type of prejudice. Atticus draws the scorn of the town because he speaks honestly about the lies they are propagating with their political power, religious dogma, and social codes—his truth telling is intolerable to them. Think about it for a moment: only those in the majority are able to deem what is politically correct. For that very reason, political correctness is a most dangerous weapon. While it once may have served its purpose in advancing dialogue and compassion, it has been reduced (by the power of politicians and mass media) to a form of demonization that marginalizes people in the way it was once intended to protect them. The last thing we need is one more weapon that stunts the little bit of true dialogue that ever takes place in the violent language of politics. In the dialogue of compassion, true biblical communication, we must feel free to have an honest exchange of ideas without being accosted or reduced to a caricature. Telling the truth, or at least sharing our perspectives on it, is the model of how we accomplish the aims of self-governance. Consider these two quotes I came across recently:

> In an innovative society, people must be free to take unpopular positions, disagree with conventional wisdom, know they are safe to challenge abuses of authority.[1]

> The truth does not require a majority to prevail, ladies and gentlemen. The truth is its own power. The truth will out. Never forget that.[2]

Both lines are eerily similar; they are espousing the same belief, and yet they are spoken by people who are on polar opposites of the political spectrum: Hillary Clinton and Rush Limbaugh. I am betting that they might never sit across a table from one another. Atticus is not concerned with the social ramifications of his beliefs. Martin Luther King Jr., Gandhi, and Nelson Mandela— all espoused beliefs not deemed acceptable to their popular ruling cultures, yet their bold truthfulness advanced the way we see the world. As people of faith, we have a responsibility to honesty, to the truth of the gospel, and should not be deterred by what the prevalent culture deems acceptable.

The second form of correctness that limits the truth and is even more damaging is religious correctness. This is demonstrated by the churchgoing folks throughout the novel. The most egregious example of this is the religious talk of the Maycomb ladies at their Missionary Tea. Mrs. Merriweather, the ringleader of the living room meeting, begins speaking about her African-American servant, who has been sulking in the aftermath of the Tom Robinson conviction. With a sense of religious satisfaction and piety, Mrs. Merriweather recounts how she told Sophy that Jesus Christ never went around sulking or complaining about life. The offensiveness of her words in this scene is remarkable; she is speaking down to a member of the town's African-American community who must be devastated by the injustice of the Tom Robinson verdict. Mrs. Meriwether follows up with the prideful affirmation, "I'll tell you, Gertrude, you never ought to let an opportunity go by to witness for the Lord" (24). The women of the Maycomb tea have adopted their culture's racism as a part of their faith and are actually supporting it with their religious-speak.

Religious correctness happens when we support the systems of politics and culture ahead of the gospel message. God delivers quite the warning about speaking for Him in the Ten Commandments. "Thou shall not take the Lord God's name in vain" is too often thought of as a reference to cursing. The Hebrew understanding of the command has far more to do what we espouse in God's name. It might read, "Don't speak for God, and don't use God's name to influence people to your own benefit." Religious correctness to me is the worst dishonesty. The women of Maycomb demonstrate that the church can become just one more institution that supports the evil of racism.

Looking Straight Through the Window: Avoiding Gossip in Our Communication

Miss Stephanie Crawford is proclaimed by our narrator to be the town gossip. Her primary role as a character in the novel is to perpetuate the scandal of Maycomb. She is responsible for spreading most of the conspicuous conjectures about the nature of the Radley family, sounds the alarm on the Finch street about the children's conspicuous presence at the trial of Tom Robinson, and is the first to recount, with animated drama, the confrontation at the post office between Bob Ewell and Atticus. It is apparent that she does a considerable amount of damage to the reputation of Boo Radley, the mysterious recluse whose shadow provides the mystery of the novel. But her rantings about him roaming around at night no doubt contribute to the community's fear of him. Scout recounts the scene when Jem recites the gossip of Miss Stephanie, "Miss Stephanie Crawford said she woke up in the middle of the night one time and saw him looking straight through the window at her . . . said his head was like a skull lookin' at her" (1). While Stephanie Crawford definitely provides some entertainment in the novel (and is scoffed at by reasonable adults like Atticus and Maudie), her rumor-mongering is harmful. (Interestingly, it is referenced a time or two in the novel that Miss Stephanie is a closet alcoholic; I always imagine that this is implicit with her unhappiness as a person, which may be borne out by the way she imposes her unhappiness on others through gossip.)

Gossip might be our most devastating form of communication. It is the extreme opposite of communicative connection. It is the whispers on the periphery outside of our subject's hearing. Gossip, in practice, implies an absence of true relationship. We use it to control and define those by whom we feel threatened or jealous. The danger of its destructive power is found not just in its absence of compassion, but in the relative obscurity with which it can be delivered and the way it can be used to maintain our oppression over others. There are too many references to the evils of gossip in the biblical narrative to list. The apostle Paul categorizes gossip with some relatively weighty forms of sinfulness: "They have become filled with every kind of wickedness, evil, greed and depravity. They are full of envy, murder, strife, deceit and malice. They are gossips" (Rom. 1:29, NIV).

I have seen the cruelty of gossip ruin the lives of young teenagers, force pastors out of their ministries, teachers out of their jobs, and marriages into counseling. It is in no way conducive to building the type of relational community we are responsible to bring the world. Consider the topics of conversation at happy hour with your friends or around the dinner table with your spouse. It is easy to catch yourself discussing someone else's life with detachment, simply because he is not present to refute what is being said. This is one of our greatest communicative challenges as people of faith. When we get together with our old friends, it is easy to reduce the conversation to gossip about one person's job or another's marriage. I think the key to defeating this type of destructive conversation lies in the simple practice of imagining the subject of the discussion as present with you. My wife and I have begun a practice of applying that to our conversations about people: would we really talk about them in that way if they were here in the room with us? Certainly discussing friends is natural and harmless. It is when our intent to hurt or malign the other is implied that it becomes gossip.

This Is Still Our Home: Building Community Through Our Communication

The ethic that Atticus lives out in his communication is one of connection and compassion toward his community. At the outset of taking the Tom Robinson case, he sits his daughter Scout down to discuss the situation. He tells her, "But remember this, no matter how bitter things get, they're still our friends and this is still our home" (9). This line illuminates why Atticus communicates with people the way he does. It is his deep understanding of his relation to the people of Maycomb that acts as the compass, guiding the tones, the volume, and the nature of his conversations with them. This character, more than any other, practices community as an ethic, as a responsibility. As I read *To Kill a Mockingbird* I am always taken aback at his ability to deal with people in this manner. Atticus abhors the racism, the lack of compassion, and the violence that permeates Maycomb. But I believe he is deeply attentive to the power of human associations and relationships. His communication with people leaves the door of influence open. His ethic concedes the disagreement with his neighbors, but maintains the connection that can allow him to bring about change in their lives through relationship—by his example. This type of communication is truly one of the deepest forms of compassion practiced by our protagonist in the novel.

It is my hope that we would all be profoundly aware of the capacity of our language to help or to heal those around us. In a culture enthralled with the power of the final say, enamored with the thrill of having the last word, captivated by the clout of being right, this ordinary lawyer from a small town in Alabama models for us something completely different. He presents an ethic of communicating that is more divine than we imagine at first glance. We speak of a God who put on human skin and walked around in it, a God of understanding and compassion who leaves the door open to relationship with us. So should we always be vigilant to avoid using language that closes the doors of redemption to others. Atticus Finch affirms to us, and *To Kill a Mockingbird* reminds us, that it is the mission and deepest responsibility of the words we use to communicate hope, to spread truth, to be agents of grace and change to the hearts of our fellow men and women, and to speak God's reality of compassion into the souls of our neighbors.

Afterword: Compassion in Action

A Conclusion . . . Or a Beginning

Winter settled in on us in Ohio when I had finished writing and the colors of fall gave way to dry leaves, dead lawns, and Christmas lights glistening on evergreens down virtually every block of our neighborhood. The sounds of my children playing outside the window of my writing desk gave way to their busyness, laughter, and wrestling inside the warmth of our home. I sat poring over the manuscript with a cup of coffee one morning, considering God and Maycomb, when something outside our window caught my eye. The trees that usually filled my vision were exposed, the limbs bare and open, and for the first time in many months I noticed just over the frosted lawn what the fallen foliage had exposed: I realized I could actually see my neighbor's home from my window. It was a curious revelation that seemed to hold me in that moment.

I reflected that the green leaves of the creative process of writing had aged to gold and floated away to return another season. Without the decorations of new words, fresh growth, the colors of new ideas, like the tree outside, I was left with the branches and structure of what I had written; and while I had intended the Parable of the Last Word to be just that, the end of the book, it suddenly seemed apparent that I needed to offer a conclusion of sorts: someplace to travel with meaning beyond these pages.

I thought about how isolation from our neighbors is the result of sin and how this issue is addressed in the themes of *To Kill a Mockingbird*—and also how it was the driving force behind God's visit to earth as a human being. I considered the truth I had encountered in recent studies and surveys that reflected how many people in today's culture view Christians as generally self-righteous, judgmental, and intolerant—a far cry from the definitions of the One we claim to follow. I was reminded of a line I'd read recently: "a community that . . . truly hears the stories of the crucified Jesus will of necessity remain open to the outsiders and strangers of the world."[1] The true purpose of *The Mockingbird Parables* is simply the essence of the gospel, the call to put compassion into action: to walk out our front doors and endeavor to truly know and love each other. In the same way we believe in a God who not only moved onto our street, but put on human skin and walked around in it, the point of each parable herein is to model that divine example—to find a way to *be a better neighbor*.

I meditated for a while on the emergence of this clear view of my own neighbor, provided by the winter tree. Isn't that what we all need? A way to allow the "leaves" that cover and hide us from each other to fall away, to somehow find a way to see, to know, and to connect with our neighbors? Yes, for those of us who serve a God who moved into our neighborhood, I believe that is our mission.

It is time to put your compassion to action, and I've gathered some resources for you to do so at mockingbirdparables.com. I hope that something you have discovered in these pages will motivate you to go to the site and use those resources to advance the message of the gospel through compassion, to be so consumed with that compassion that you cease to view others as outsiders and begin to recognize them for who they really are: your neighbors. It is my desire for you to fervently take part in the invasion of light that occurred two thousand years ago on a lonely hill—to rediscover something that all of us have lost: what it truly means to be a good neighbor.

For more information visit: Compassion in Action at mockingbirdparables.com.

Parable Reflections

Boo Radley: Discovering Our Divine Mysterious Neighbor
- Consider how questions have played a role in your most meaningful relationships and adventures. When is the last time you pursued a question about God?
- What is your definition of God? If you were to draw a picture of God, what would He look like? Does your idea or definition of God encourage you to pursue Him?
- How often do you take the time to notice God in the everydayness of your life? Do you really believe that God is pursuing you? Do you really see God as a compassionate neighbor?

House Fires and Church Collections:
Our Responsibility to Care for the Neighborhood
- If God has truly invited us into His home, how should this affect the way we treat others?
- When is the last time you considered what it would be like to "walk around in someone else's skin"? How might this encourage you to be a better neighbor?
- What are some practical ways you might go about caring for those in your own neighborhood?

Scout Finch: The Role of Women in Faith

- Consider what expectations you have for people of the opposite gender? How do your expectations of others affect the way you interact with them?
- Do you believe the Bible defines specific roles for women to play in the church? How might this conflict with your own beliefs?
- How can I empower my neighbors to be free from the expectations of others?

Miss Maudie's Azaleas: Our Responsibility to Care for Creation

- How can spending time in nature enhance your relationship with God? With your family?
- How can we learn more about God and ourselves spending time outdoors?
- Consider some practical ways that you can become a more responsible steward of creation?

Atticus Finch: The Model of Christian Courage

- Consider the daily decisions you make in your own life. Are they courageous? How do you define courage in your everyday life?
- How does your faith affect or transform your definition of courage?
- Do you really allow your belief in the resurrection to define the way you live your life?

*The Missionary Tea: Our Responsibility to the Global
Neighborhood Begins at Home*

- What does it mean to demonstrate true compassion for
  those in your own church community?
- How might confession and transparency in your own
  community enable you to be compassionate?
- Consider the practical ways you might response to the
  needs of the global community.

*The Great Depression: The Christian Ethic
of Financial Responsibility*

- How consumed are you with acquiring material and
  wealth—really?
- Sit down and examine your bank statements. Where do
  you spend your money? What do you truly value?
- How can you commit your own resources to helping others?

*Tom Robinson: How Compassion Can Overcome Our
Differences*

- How do you view people of other denominations, races,
  social classes, or religions?
- What does God really have to say about justice? How can
  you work to become more compassionate to those who are
  different?
- Consider what you can do practically to pursue
  righteousness through compassion.
- How can you work to make Sundays less segregated?

Raising Jem and Scout: Parenting for Compassion
- How can we model compassion to our children?
- How can you respond to the dire need for role models, foster parents, and mentors in the lives of children?
- Do you see discipline as teaching or punishment?
- How can you prioritize your life to focus on your children?

The Last Word: Communicating to Build Community
- Reflect on your most recent conversations. In what ways was your language life-giving?
- How can you respond more clearly to your obligation to tell the truth?
- In what situations do you most often put your needs, your voice, and your opinion ahead of others? Reflect on the emotions or feelings that cause that type of communication? How can you change it?
- What are some practical ways to avoid gossip?
- How often are you cognizant and prayerful about the power of your words?

Acknowledgments

This book about compassion, the power of story, and what it means to love your neighbor is a work that has been lovingly formed through my own community—those far away and near, those living among us and dear ones who have passed on. I am thankful for your friendship, your prayers, for the roles you have played in my story. I am a grateful participant, and I feel eternally blessed and indebted to you all . . .

To my wife, Kristy, who will always be more than I deserve: thank you for your encouragement and love, and all of your hours of patience through the process of this book.

To Noah, Eli, Jake, and Raegan: thank you for your patience with me as I disappeared to my writing to play "Boo Radley" for so many weeks. I love to write and to teach, but I will always love you much more. You all make my life beautiful.

To Mom and David: thank you for your advice, and for loaning out your kitchen table as my writing space. Mom, thank you for your encouragement, and your willingness to listen to each and every line of my writing. To my brother, Zach: our long conversations about God and story and literature have helped shape my writing and my life.

To my friends in the ministry, Chet Bush and Chris Bean: our long conversations and your persistent encouragement and prayers have been a priceless gift to me throughout this process. To my friends in publishing, Preston and Paul, thank you for pushing me to begin this journey. To my family and very good friends who have prayed for me and encouraged me through this process: I am grateful for each and every one of you.

To my agent, Kyle Olund: thank you for your support, friendship, and persistence. To my editor, Jamie Chavez: I am incredibly grateful for your skill and wisdom in helping me shape this work into a book. To Joel and Kristen at Nelson: thanks for believing in this project.

To the educators who inspired me: Dr. Ruth Cook, for helping me discover the joy and divinity of literature; to Dr. Tim Green, for engaging my imagination in the greatest story ever told—the biblical narrative; and *especially* to Dr. George Kersey, for encouraging me to write and modeling for me so clearly how the power of one word can change a person's life.

Finally, to Harper Lee: thank you for capturing all our imaginations with such a beautiful work of art. To me, there has never been a more moving and honest American story written.

Notes

To Kill a Mockingbird and the Power of Parables

1. Transcription by author from Dead Poets Society, Tom Schulman, screenwriter (Touchstone Pictures, 1989).

2. Bernhard W. Anderson, *The Unfolding Drama of the Bible* (Minneapolis: Augsburg Fortress Publishers, 2006), 10.

3. Harper Lee, "Love—In Other Words," *Vogue* 137, 15 April 1961, 64–5.

4. Eugene H. Peterson, *Eat This Book: A Conversation in the Art of Spiritual Reading* (Cambridge: Wm. B. Eerdmans Publishing Co., 2006), 11.

5. Dallas Willard, *The Divine Conspiracy: Rediscovering Our Hidden Life In God* (New York: HarperCollins, 1998), 281.

6. C. S. Lewis, *The Weight of Glory* (New York: HarperCollins, 1949), 45.

Boo Radley: Discovering Our Divine Mysterious Neighbor

1. Anne Lamott, "God doesn't take sides," Salon.com, 27 April 2005, http://www.salon.com/opinion/feature/2005/04/27/gods_warning_signs/index.html (accessed 4 Nov. 2009).

House Fires and Church Collections: Our Responsibility to Care for the Neighborhood

1. Dietrich Bonhoeffer, Geffrey B. Kelly, Daniel W. Bloesch, James H. Burtness, *Life Together: Prayerbook of the Bible* (Fortress, 2005), 36.

Scout Finch: The Role of Women in Faith

1. John and Stasi Eldredge, *Captivating: Unveiling the Mystery of a Woman's Soul* (Nashville: Thomas Nelson, 2005).

2. Pliny the Younger, *Epistulae X.96.*

3. Eugene Peterson, "Introduction Galatians," *The Message* (Colorado Springs: NavPress, 2002), 2113.

Miss Maudie's Azaleas: Our Responsibility to Care for Creation

1. Wendell Berry, "A Few Words in Favor of Edward Abbey," *What Are People For?: Essays* (New York: North Point Press, 1990).

2. Ralph Waldo Emerson, "Art," *Essays, First Series*, 1841.

3. William Wordsworth, "The Tables Turned," 1888.

4. Linford Detweiler, "Letter From Over the Rhine, July 15, 2009," The Orchard, a blog, 20 July 2009, www.overtherhine.com/orchard/index. php?showtopic=9034&st=0&p=251214&#entry251214, (accessed 5 Dec. 2009).

5. Wendell Berry, "A Practical Harmony," *What Are People For?: Essays* (New York: North Point Press, 1990).

6. Wendell Berry, "A Native Hill," *The Art of the Commonplace: The Agrarian Essays of Wendell Berry* (Berkley, CA: Counterpoint, 2002).

Atticus Finch: The Model of Christian Courage

1. "'Mockingbird' Hero Honored in Monroeville," *Birmingham News* (Alabama), 3 May 1997.

The Great Depression: The Christian Ethic of Financial Responsibility

1. Quoted in Richard J. Foster, *Celebration of Discipline: The Path to Spiritual Growth* (New York: HarperCollins, 1978), 15.

2. You can see a transcription of this speech (given 4 Mar. 1933) at History Matters, historymatters.gmu.edu/d/5057/ (accessed 27 November 2009); it was published in Samuel Rosenman, ed., *The Public Papers of Franklin D. Roosevelt, Volume Two: The Year of Crisis, 1933* (New York: Random House, 1938), 11–16.

3. Dave Ramsey, *The Total Money Makeover: A Proven Plan for Financial Fitness* (Nashville, TN: Thomas Nelson, 2003), 19.

4. Walter Brueggemann, *The Prophetic Imagination, Second Edition* (Minneapolis, MN: Augsberg Fortress, 2001), 1.

5. Bono, Keynote Address, speaking at the 54th National Prayer Breakfast, the Hilton Washington Hotel, 2 Feb. 2006; transcript available at speakingoffaith.publicradio.org/programs/evangelicalevolution/bono-prayerbreakfast.shtml (accessed 27 Nov. 2009).

Tom Robinson: How Compassion Can Overcome Our Differences

1. Frederick Buechner, *The Hungering Dark* (New York, NY: HarperCollins Publishers, 1969), 50.

2. Ellen Levine, *Freedom's Children: Young Civil Rights Activists Tell Their Own Stories* (New York: Penguin Group, 1993), 11–12.

3. Ibid., 6.

Raising Jem and Scout Finch: Parenting for Compassion

1. Robert Fulghum, *It Was On Fire When I Lay Down On It* (New York: Villard, 1989).

The Last Word: Communicating to Build Community

1. Hillary Rodham Clinton, in a speech to students in Moscow, Russia, 14 Oct. 2009; reported in Matthew Lee, "Hillary Clinton Touts Freedom in Speech to Russian Students," Associated Press, www.cnsnews.com/news/article/55455 (accessed 28 Nov. 2009).

2. Rush Limbaugh, "Thursday Quotes: The Truth Detector!" The Rush Limbaugh Show, www.rushlimbaugh.com/home/daily/site_051409/content/01125100.guest.html (accessed 29 Nov. 2009).

Afterword: Compassion in Action

1. William C. Placher, *Narratives of a Vulnerable God* (Louisville: Wesminister John Knox Press, 1994), 155.

About the Author

Matt Litton is a writer, educator, and speaker. He completed his undergraduate work in English and Religion and holds a Master of Arts in Education from Trevecca Nazarene University in Nashville, Tennessee. Matt and his wife, Kristy, have four children: Noah, Elijah, Jakob, and Raegan.